Queen of Olympos
A Devotional Anthology
for Hera and Iuno

Second Edition

Edited by Lykeia

"HERA"
by Katherine Meyers Dickens

BIBLIOTHECA ALEXANDRINA

FOREWORD

I hope that this collection of devotional material in honor of the Queen of Olympos, Hera (also called Iuno/Juno by the Romans) brings you much joy. I also hope that it broadens your understanding of this often vilified, much misunderstood -- but historically much adored and honored -- goddess. Devotees from around the globe have come together to create this volume in celebration of our Queen, to share our knowledge and worship of her with the rest of the world. I pray that this anthology shall further facilitate such worship, and inspire further devotion.

Lykeia
July 2013

FROM THE DESK OF THE EDITOR-IN-CHIEF

A devotional in honor of the Queen of the Gods has been unofficially in the works for several years. I am proud that we at Bibliotheca Alexandrina are finally able to offer the Goddess Her rightful due.

The anthology is divided into four sections. In "Litaneia" you will find poems and prayers composed by Her modern devotees. "Mythos" contains modern tales and fables, while "Apologia" features essays and analysis of the Goddess, Her nature, and Her place in mythology, cosmology and philosophy. Finally, "Evláveia" focuses on rites and rituals in honor of the Goddess.

The poems, prayers, music, artwork, essays and short fiction which fill the pages of this anthology honor the Goddess in all Her ferocity, wonder, and complexity. She is not a Goddess easily understood or defined -- and She is most definitely not a Goddess to be boxed into the category of "shrewish wife." Here, you will find a Goddess regal and intimidating, loving and compassionate, wise and angry -- a Goddess truly worthy of Her role as Queen of Olympos.

Rebecca Buchanan

TABLE OF CONTENTS

DEDICATION

DELIAN HYMN IV
by Callimachus

Honored Hera,
most eminent of goddesses,
I am yours,
everything is yours,
you sit lawful ruler of olympos;
we fear no other female hand.
Dearest one,
defend your slaves,
lady,
who walk the earth at your command.

"QUEEN OF OLYMPOS"
by Lykeia

LITANEIA

A WEDDING SONG
by Jessica Orlando

Juno Interduca

Lead the bride to her waiting mate

Beneath the arch, 'tween the garlands wound

Place their hands together in ties that bind,

See them off into their fate

Flowers fall, the winds blow true

Good wishes and many blessings

May they fall unto you

Juno Domiduca

Lead the bride to the waiting house

Help it to become her home

A shelter from the furor of the world

A hearth ever burning with warmth and light

Prosperity to this family

Good wishes and many blessings

May they fall unto you

Juno Cinxia

Lead the bride to her wedding bed

Lift her veil and show her the way

Give her freedom and curiosity always

Let her learn the pleasure of her new mate

To find the love that holds them true

Good wishes and many blessings

May they fall unto you

Good wishes and many blessings

May they fall unto you

A Wedding Song

Lyrics by Jessica Orlando
Music by Raven Kaldera

ADORATIONS OF JUNO

by P. Sufenas Virius Lupus

I adore you, Juno Capitolina,

> foremost of Roman goddesses.

I adore you, Juno Sospita,

> savior of the Roman state.

I adore you, Juno Caelestis,

> speaker of oracles in Carthage.

I adore you, Juno Sororia,

> protectress of girls becoming women.

I adore you, Juno Caprotina,

> fertile protectress of serving-women.

I adore you, Juno Sispes,

> raven-shielded, snake-speared goddess of Lanuvium.

I adore you, Juno Curitis,

> spear-goddess of chariot and shield.

I adore you, Juno Regina,

> queen of gods and men.

I adore you, Juno Lucetia,

> bringer of light by torch or sun.

I adore you, Juno Quiritis,

matron of laws and assemblies.

I adore you, Juno Lucina,

grove-goddess bringing children from the womb.

I adore you, Juno Populona,

mother of the people, patroness of soldiers.

I adore you, Juno Martialis,

celebrated in the month of March.

I adore you, Juno Perusina,

goddess who motivates emperors in dream.

I adore you, Juno Mater,

mother-goddess of Italy.

I adore you, Juno Opigena,

daughter of abundance, aider of childbirth.

I adore you, Juno Moneta,

warner with geese, assurance of currency.

I adore you, Juno Dea,

great goddess in all her forms.

ROYAL HERA
(A WEDDING INVOCATION)
by Diane "Emerald" Bronowicz

Wife of the Thunderer -- Ruler of the Heavens, Goddess of Women, and Queen of the Gods.

We call upon you this day as the Protectress of the sacred state of matrimony. While

Aphrodite rocks us with tremors of desire, you help us lay the stable foundations of home

and hearth that will nurture and protect our relationship throughout the years, weathering

all the storms we face together. Honored Hera, we ask that you bless this marriage with

a home found in each other, sheltering and sustaining our love until death parts us.

Hera Gamelia: Hail!

LOVE AND COMMITMENT
by Melia Suez

I used to believe

love is all in a relationship

everything else would follow

naturally in succession

I want to believe

part of me fights to believe

how foolish.

how naive

how childish

Glorious Aphrodite's gifts

catalysts for a relationship

respect, like, lust, love, need

relationship roots, these are

non-sustaining on their own

survival beyond

sunny days of laughter

through the rain of tears

through dark nights of uncertainty

through torments of jealousy, anger

takes commitment

Aphrodite's emotional package

her hormonal urges

are a house of cards on their own

another is required for a solid frame

one known for her patience,

her commitment in good times and bad

Passionate, Determined Hera

All the love in the world

contained within one relationship

will wither and die

when the excitement is gone

when the newness wears off

weeks, months, years can go by

yet if commitment isn't there

neither will the relationship

only a farce that disappears

in the gentlest of breezes

Jealous Hera

terrible the acts

of a jealous heart

jealousy is a warning

lines are down, no dial tone

prompt resolution

tools of patience and compromise

nasty necessary compromises

leaving all pleased, disappointed

yet the sign of commitment

requiring a bit selflessness

As the selfish are committed

Only to themselves

Hail Aphrodite!

May your gifts keep the heart pumping!

Hail Hera!

May your gifts be the glue

that keeps it strong and healthy!

ZAS AND KHTHONIE

by Melia Suez

Zas, King of Olympus, Divine Craftsman,

once set aside his transforming bolt

for a surprisingly domestic task …

an intricate weaving of astonishing beauty

adorned with land and sea, rivers and trees,

mountains and meadows, plants and animals.

A wondrous gift but not just any gift,

a wedding gift for his bride, Khthonie,

Queen of Tartarus, Ruler of Primordial Matter.

At first it was the blanket on their nuptial bed,

under which pleasure was given and received.

When they reluctantly left their chambers,

Zas wrapped his beloved in his handiwork

addressing her as Gaia, Fount of Life,

Like the Tree of Life, the Winged Oak,

her toes are securely rooted in the underworld,

while her horned crown shines in the heavens

pouring ambrosia for our immortal souls.

Such a union produced a golden bond

light as air and heavy as chains.

In loving joy, a fertile cloud is produced

bringing growth wherever it blankets.

In anger, unbreakable chains are forged

Giving advantage to the one on high

leaving the depths suspended, whipped

like any common malcontent or slave.

Distinctly separate yet inseparably unified,

Earth and Sky, Khthonie and Zas.

PRAYER TO HERA
by Hearthstone

To peerless Hera, gracious queen of the heavens,

I offer my praise. Hera most fair, most beguiling,

most delightful of goddesses, beloved bride

of resounding Zeus, great and noble of bearing,

crowned in brightest gold, bearer of the lotus staff.

O deep-eyed goddess who sits enthroned in glory,

whose temples once stood tall across the old lands,

whose name was sung by poets, whose tales were told

in theater and hall, abundant your blessings,

terrible your wrath, in the hearts of men you kindle

the finest of feeling, the firmest of faith.

Hera, I call to you with words of devotion.

POEM TO HERA
by Jonathan Agathokles

O Cow-eyed Hera, Resplendent Queen,

Whose regal might can by all be seen,

Who rules the Gods and mortal men,

Beautious and wrathful, again and again!

Born to Rhea as Daughter of Kronos,

But by the design of Ge and Ouranos,

Was released from ill fate by Mighty Zeus,

Who freed his siblings, who set them loose.

Once he saw you he burned with desire,

He fell in love and wished to acquire

You as his beloved and eternal spouse,

Sharing with you his bed and his house.

Thus it is that you became

Patron of marriage, of unending fame,

Protectress of the blushing brides,

In whom every one of them confides.

O Loud-Thundering Zeus's splendid wife,

Mother of rain, who nourishes life,

Whom Gods and Men hold in the Highest Renown,

You are adorned with jewels and a golden crown!

I pray this poem has been pleasing,

To You, O Golden-Throned Queen of All,

May Your blessings be ever-increasing,

O Mistress who holds all in thrall!

JUNO AT LULLINGSTONE
by P. Sufenas Virius Lupus

INVIDA SI TAURI VIDISSET IUNO NATATUS

IUSTIUS AEOLIAS ISSET AD USQUE DOMOS

"If jealous Juno had seen the swimming of the bull

she might more justly have gone to the house of Aeolus."*

Fly, Bellerophon, and do not stay your spear

when the Chimaera comes face-to-face with you.

I wish that your sons had not stayed their spears at Sarpedon

when he was a boy, son of either Europa or Laodameia, but
   certainly Zeus —

that whoremongering philanderer! Had Sarpedon fallen then,

Zeus' tears of blood would have fallen upon Mount Ida

and stained the radiant thighs of young Ganymede red,

shielding them from the wandering eyes of my husband...

but no, he saw him and snatched him, sent Hebe from our hall,

and stirred my anger at all the descendants of Tros.

Instead, Sarpedon fell in battle with Patroklos, Achilleus' boy,

and the defeat of that city of famed walls followed, thus Aeneas

made his voyage, and I went to Aeolus' lofty citadel

20

to ask his favors in stirring winds against sails.

Aeneas' great-grandson, Brutus, came to this isle with his
Trojans.

O legacy of slaughter, o curse of Ganymede's kin!

May this house and all its inhabitants receive my favor

for honoring me as their foundation-stone through all seasons

when the island itself falls and falls again like Troy of old.

*These lines are on a floor mosaic at a villa in Lullingstone,
England. They allude to the first book of Vergil's Aeneid, and
are seen above an image of Europa on a bull with two cupids
over the sea. An adjoining panel shows Bellerophon on a
Pegasus attacking the Chimaera with a border of the four
Seasons. I have connected these images to their legitimate
mythological roots, and added the British myth of their island's
founder at the end in Hera/Juno's narrative.

66 Adorations to Juno
by Galina Krasskova

I adore You, Mother of Rome.

I adore You, Who protects Your people.

I adore You, Mighty Queen.

I adore You, Wife of Jupiter.

I adore You, of the Capitoline Triad.

I adore You, Born aloft by the peacock.

I adore You, Fierce in war.

I adore You, Beautiful One.

I adore You, of the goatskin cloak.

I adore You, Goddess of vital power.

I adore You, Goddess of Renewal.

I adore You, Who brings Aid to Your supplicants.

I adore You, Rejuvenator.

I adore You, Goddess of marriage.

I adore You, Patroness of brides.

I adore You, Sovereign Power.

I adore You, Mater Regina.

I adore You, Bringer of Light, Lucina.

I adore You, Friend to women.

I adore You, Friend to warriors, too.

I adore You, Who delights in heroes.

I adore You, Rich in valor.

I adore You, Who hears the cries of Your people.

I adore You, Who guards the community against destruction.

I adore You, Who brings increase.

I adore You, Who watches over the army.

I adore You, Goddess of military might.

I adore You, Generous One.

I adore You, Goddess of cycles.

I adore You, Goddess of Heaven's Power.

I adore You, Who presides over birth.

I adore You, Who strengthens Your people.

I adore You, Goddess of beginnings.

I adore You, to Whom sacrifices are given.

I adore You, Delight of many temples.

I adore You, Goddess of the kalends.

I adore You, Covella.

I adore You, Moneta.

I adore You, Wise in political maneuvering.

I adore You, Goddess of Power.

I adore You, Goddess of governance.

I adore You, Patroness of Lupercalia.

I adore You, Goddess of expiation.

I adore You, Purifier.

I adore You, Whose Power averts destruction.

I adore You, Whose glance wards against grievous harm.

I adore You, Preserver of marriage.

I adore You, Preserver of all sacred rites.

I adore You, Defender.

I adore You, Sospita, Savior of Your people.

I adore You, Goddess of passages.

I adore You, Goddess of fertility.

I adore You, Beloved of Your people.

I adore You, to Whom the fig is sacred.

I adore You, Beloved of soldiers,

      invoked by those going to war.

I adore You, Patroness of the Curia.

I adore You, Who shakes the spear aloft.

I adore You, Who warns of danger.

I adore You, Who protects the home.

I adore You, Who blesses Your worshippers.

I adore You, Goddess of our ancestors.

I adore You, Who brings all good things to fruition.

I adore You, of Whom the poets sing.

I adore You, Majestic, Magnificent,

    Mighty Goddess.

I adore You, Juno.

HERA MEGALA METER

by P. Sufenas Virius Lupus

Gaia, Rhea, Demeter are heralded by all

as the Great Mothers of gods and men --

but what of I, queen of the gods and wife of Zeus?

Only a small number of children are called mine:

Ares, Hephaistos, Hebe, Eileithyia, Ate, Eris, and Typhon.

Little do gods and mortals know, however,

how many of these children are truly of Zeus.

Only Eileithyia, ironically, is the seed of her father;

Hebe and Hephaistos, Ares and Typhon are mine alone

(though the gods only reckon the latter as such, my curse

to never produce solely again lest the consequence be worse),

and Ate and Eris are the seed of an interloper:

the goddess Nyx who envelopes all the heavens when she comes.

On those nights of passion when the Thunderer foolishly felt

he was most in ecstasy and virile perfection

it was Nyx within and over him, overcoming him,

that gave him the vigor to engender the twins,

the mother of strife and the force of delusion … appropriate.

No suitor has survived to sue for my love, sought or not by me;

but in the quiet of evening when the king sleeps,

Metis speaks to me from his innards and tells me of the children

who would have been born had the suitors succeeded.

Had Kreios, Koios, Hyperion, and Iapetos all in white gypsum

not been destroyed by Zeus for the death of Zagreus

I would have borne them a mighty race of titanic heroes;

though Lelantos was never seen by Zeus, he panicked and fled,

but I would have given birth to twins by him: Harpokrates and
Hesychia,

and on a later visit, a youthful god called Antinous;

Ixion failed to rape me, but if he were not wheel-bound in
punishment

our child would have been Ekdeës, who would fail to conquer
Troy;

and if Jason, my most favored, had not married Medea, our son
Autoteleiotes

would have averted war between the Achaeans and the Trojans.

Though men and gods do not call me "Great Mother"

may they realize in their mind's silence and their heart's fear

that I, queen of the gods, am mother all-powerful.

JUNO REGINA CAELESTIS

by P. Sufenas Virius Lupus

Sing my praises, O people of Carthage,

and carry my songs in your sad defeat

to the ears of your conquerors, the Romans,

when they salt the earth before building my temples.

The Great Mother of Phrygia aids them

in turning the tides against you in war,

but I desert the honors you have given me

for a brighter future in a city of seven hills.

I look forward to the time when a distant lover,

Jupiter of Doliche, best and greatest,

will join with me in a holy union

known only to initiates of our mysteries.

Juno, Queen of the Heavens

will have her name sung for generations

beyond the falling of empires and temples

on continents unknown even to Carthage.

HERA
by Lykeia

Between the light and misty remains

Of crystalline drops of heavenly rains,

The form of which to your messenger imbues

Gentle and swift, fair Iris of myriad hues,

A bright arch, your bridge across the sky

For your gentle rain, as if the heaven in joy did cry,

Brings your beauteous gifts upon the earth

The blushing flowers reaching up from the stony girth.

For never more do the larks so sweetly sing

Than after the silvery cuckoo shakes his wings,

And the raindrops falling from his feather-tips

To land upon your children's parted lips.

In these fashions you send us your motherly love

Delivered in plenty from the bright sky above.

HYMN TO HERA TELKHINIA

by Lykeia

Hail Telkhinia, storm-riding, O undaunted, ravaging one

You who shine with the beauty of dew, lit by the sun,

As from the drops of rain that slide across your breast

Luminously gleam and shine, there does Iris manifest

To follow the clamorous roar of your brazen-hooved team

As from your regal locks ever-shining droplets stream

Billowing behind you from the fan of the cuckoo's wings

As he darts around you, through the gusty rain he brings,

For the cuckoo you long ago received to your arms

As he happily captivated you to your husband's charms

Who, ever in merriment, steals the kiss of breath from your lips

When from his rain-sweet mouth you take rapturous sips.

For as the fern unfurls her fronds to receive the blessed rain

So amid the clouds where among thunder you have often lain

You open yourself to him, and all around the storms blow,

Let your storm bring the nourishing rain from above to below,

Be so softly driven by your love and not by angry tempests grow.

To Hera
by Lykeia

Muses join me upon the hill, and lift your harmonious voices high

As we sing to the goddess, golden-browed Hera, heavenly queen.

She who sits high-throned in the company of the radiant gods,

And is adored by the great-plumed, bright-crested birds at her hand.

Hail to the heavenly queen who blesses the marriage-bed,

And there the morning-dewed bride receives the nuptial kiss.

Revered goddess, hear the songs and prayers of women who entreat,

Accept the welcomed place of honor at our home and hearth.

Your own house receives you, and will tremble before your might,

And too you ease the head of your spouse against your pillowed breast.

Most honorable Hera you are strong-armed among gods and men,

Your will rises like a lioness from the earth's plumage draping the land.

As terrible as your might, you coax with your honeyed tongue,

The wearied husband to your fragrant arms upon the mountain peak.

And there with Aphrodite's grace, do you extend your loving embrace,

Amends are made and cordiality restored between husband and wife.

Good counselor of the king among gods and men, veiled goddess,

Your utterance commands the attention of all in great assembly.

Hyperkheiria, your hand extends throughout the heaven's arch,

The stars and moon in orbit shine upon your heavenly form.

The hours, days and passing seasons bring forth your holy cup,

As you swallow the great libations that pass through your pearly lips.

PRAYER TO HERA, EILEITHYIA AND ARTEMIS
by Lykeia

Hail to Hera, Hail Queenly goddess of mothers, hail to you!

O Hail to you, who blesses the oikos with generations new,

Bestower of heirs, of laudable sons and daughters true,

Ever turn your kindly gaze upon we who give adoration to you,

And protect our women in their travail that marriage sew.

Hail to you Hera, mother of Eileithyia, mother of Artemis

May our oikos know ever the happiness of continuation's bliss.

Hail to you Eileithyia, Hail to you O Hastener of the womb!

Hail to you O Midwife, you who loosens the tight bloom,

Drawing forth by your light, O bringer of mercy and relief,

The children of this oikos in generations, like so many a leaf

Budding ever anew upon our family's far-reaching tree,

That never shall our oikos be washed away by time's great sea

Nor lost forever to memory; may you ever impart your aid.

Hail to you Artemis, Hail to you O Great Nurse of all!

Hail to you who delights in the babe's first lusty squall

You who gentles the harsh grief of a mother's labor pains

As your light, O Prothyria, over the babe ever kindly reigns,

Protecting the doorway of the succession of our tender young

And nourishing them from the divine fountain of life, sprung

From among the eternal gods; may your arrows ever protect them.

Hail to Hera, Hail to Eileithyia, Hail to Artemis, maiden of the door

Hail to you O Goddesses, may you smile upon us ever more.

HYMN TO LESBIAN HERA
by Rebecca Buchanan

Atop our highest peak

We have set an altar for you

Mistress Hera

Most Glorious Goddess

Most Famous

Most Benevolent

And beside yours

Altars for the Suppliant's God

and the God Who Devours Deer Raw

But for you

Mother of All

First and highest praise

(after Alkaios)

ADORATIONS TO HERA
by Aldrin Fauni-Tanos

I adore you, Hera.

I adore you, undoubted queen.

I adore you, splendid daughter of Rheia and Kronos.

I adore you, grandchild of broad-breasted Gaia and wide-arching Ouranos.

I adore you, sister and wife of loud-thundering Zeus.

I adore you, mother of peerless Ares.

I adore you, mother of youthful Hebe.

I adore you, mother of skillful Hephaistos.

I adore you, foster-mother of many gods.

I adore you, born in Samos.

I adore you, raised in Argos.

I adore you, mother of cows.

I adore you, mother of people.

I adore you, nourishing one.

I adore you, fertile one.

I adore you, abundant and gracious.

I adore you, providing milk overflowing.

I adore you, lady of the pomegranate.

I adore you, lady with the lotus-staff.

I adore you, queen of heaven.

I adore you, bringer of sweet rain.

I adore you, kindler of stars.

I adore you, sending cool gales.

I adore you, shining heifer.

I adore you, dreaded lioness.

I adore you, cuckoo.

I adore you, drawn by peacocks.

I adore you, attended by the seasons.

I adore you, mother of kings.

I adore you, mother of heroes.

I adore you, source of sovereignty.

I adore you, highly crowned.

I adore you, knowing heaven and earth.

I adore you, mother of law and order.

I adore you, exalted one.

I adore you, mother of people.

I adore you, protector of women.

I adore you, patron of marriage.

I adore you, keeper of keys.

I adore you, protector at childbirth.

I adore you, keeper of harmony.

I adore you, faithful one.

I adore you, my lady, my queen, my mother.

HERA HOLY QUEEN
by Rebecca Buchanan

I sing glory to Hera,

August daughter of Rhea,

Favored of Gaea,

Mighty, resplendent, radiant as the peacock.

Your wonders are known throughout creation,

From the starry reaches of Heaven to the torturous depths of Hades.

Holy Queen,

Of you, Hera, I sing!

Six Hymns to Hera

by Rebecca Buchanan

:I:

You are the shimmering peacock

Whom Zeus knew

Before all other creatures.

Oh most beautiful, most august one.

How deep was the God's delight in You

When within You He placed

The heat of His embrace

So that by You glorious Sons and Daughters could be suckled.

What ecstasy Your womb knew

When all heaven's harmony

Rang out from You

For You bore the glorious Immortals

When Your majesty joined with God.

(after Hildegarde von Bingen)

:II:

Hera

Equal of Zeus

Queen to his King

Mother to his Father

Sister to his Brother

Heifer to his Bull

Gentle spring showers to his tempestuous storms

Seated upon her throne of golden clouds

Most eminent

Most glorious

Queen of Heaven

:III:

Queen of Spring Rains

Cuckoo atop her sceptre

     (sacred long before Zeus assumed that form)

Pomegranate in hand

     (fruit of the divine wife)

Worshipped as Child

     (unbridled)

     Wife

(flourishing)

Widow

(regal)

At Argos and Mycenae

and Olympia and

Perachora and Samos

and Sparta and

Tiryns

Hera

August Queen

Enthroned in rainbow clouds

:IV:

I sing

Hera!

August Queen of All Immortals

Granddaughter of Gaea

deep-wombed

Daughter of Rhea

mountain-lover

Mother of Ares

battle-scarred

Mother of Hebe

    ever-youthful

Mother of Hephaestus

    nimble-fingered

Mother of Eileithyia

    blood-ribboned

August Queen of All Immortals

Hera!

I sing

:V:

I

sing the

peacock queen:

iridescent

keen-eyéd beauty

:VI:

She is the great cow

her milk the

river of heaven

59 ADORATIONS TO HERA

by Galina Krasskova

I adore You, Queen of Olympus.

I adore You, Wife of Zeus.

I adore You, Daughter of Rhea.

I adore You, Daughter of Cronus.

I adore You, Goddess of women.

I adore You, Protector of marriage.

I adore You, fierce in Your power.

I adore You, Beautiful and Cow-eyed.

I adore You, Peacock Goddess.

I adore You, Enthroned One.

I adore You, Majestic One.

I adore You, Adorned with the polos.

I adore You, Well-ornamented One.

I adore You, Bestower of Blessings.

I adore You, Bringer of Gifts.

I adore You, Who Guards Your territory.

I adore You, Who forgives no slight.

I adore You, fierce in Your anger.

I adore You, Whom one does not cross.

44

I adore You, Ripe for Marriage.

I adore You, Mistress of Your House.

I adore You, Goddess of the sanctuary.

I adore You, Beloved by women.

I adore You, Ever-Renewing.

I adore You, Who blesses birthing.

I adore You, Rich in Honor.

I adore You, Who presides at weddings.

I adore You, Who maintains the home.

I adore You, of many faces.

I adore You, Bearer of the poppy.

I adore You, Bearer of the pomegranate.

I adore You, Sometimes veiled.

I adore You, Eater of Goats.

I adore You, Glorious One of the heights.

I adore You, Goddess of Argos.

I adore You, Mighty Queen.

I adore You, Whited armed Lady.

I adore You, at once Widow and Virgin.

I adore You, Goddess of the marriage bed.

I adore You, Mother of Ares.

I adore You, Mother of Hebe.

I adore You, Mother of Eris.

I adore You, Mother of Eileithyia.

I adore You, Mother of Enyo.

I adore You, Mother of Hephaistos.

I adore You, Mighty in War.

I adore You, of the Gleaming Chariot.

I adore You, Beloved of amazons.

I adore You, for Whom the hero quests.

I adore You, Bearer of serpents.

I adore You, Goad of Hercules.

I adore You, Wounded One.

I adore You, Who sends forth the gadfly.

I adore You, Mistress of the Elements.

I adore You, Goddess of the Heavens.

I adore You, Mistress of the earth.

I adore You, Whose presence consecrates.

I adore You, Ever pure.

I adore You now and forever,

Mighty Queen,

Beloved Goddess,

Hera.

HERA MY QUEEN
by Rebecca Buchanan

My Queen

Beloved of Heaven

Jeweled like the peacock

Gilded by the new spring sun

Poised at the Gates of Olympus,

       thrown wide by flower-clad Seasons --

Praise to my Heavenly Queen

Praise to my August Queen

Praise to mighty Hera

(after Enheduanna)

Hera Spring Bride

by Rebecca Buchanan

At the cry of the cuckoo

> She comes

At the fall of fertile rain

> She comes

At the blowing of gentle winds

> She comes

Hera

Spring Bride

TELÉIA

by Jennifer Lawrence

I understand you so much better now.

The stories of the gods were written by men:

Vain men, proud men, wanton and willful,

With a man's hungers, and a man's needs.

They portrayed your husband as one of themselves:

A father, a lord, a king,

With a man's hungers, and a man's needs.

Without his trysts, they say, so many Olympians and heroes

Simply would not be:

No Apollo and Artemis, no Dionysos,

No Hercules, no Perseus,

No Persephone, no Hermes,

No Graces and no Muses,

No Seasons and no Fates

Most of the seats on the heights of Mount Olympus

Would simply stand empty.

But --

From the first, you spurned his advances and ignored his pleas,

Knowing he knew nothing of fidelity;

Every gift he brought, you refused;

Every flattering compliment he whispered, you stopped your ears against.

Eventually, he sunk to trickery,

Changing his shape to beguile your pity,

And only when you had brought that half-drowned bird

Inside from the pounding storm--

(oh, if only you had recognized that warning sign!)

-- he took you by force, and when he was done,

You had no choice but to wed your brother,

Or live with the shame forever after.

Perhaps you thought that,

At least with the title of queen,

You could content yourself with respect, if not love,

But he made no effort to hide his affairs,

And you knew others knew of them, also.

The cloak of dignity you would have wrapped round yourself

Became the cuckold's tattered veil,

And all that was left to you then

Were the flames of jealousy and rage

And the icy chains of hatred.

Perhaps you could understand that the women he chose had little choice of their own --

For who could withstand the King of the Gods?

What woman could withstand his guile, or stand fast against his strength?

Nonetheless, your fury needed a target,

And you could no more strike against him, your King,

Than they could,

And so you chose to strike them down when you could --

Rewarding their illicit pleasure with death if possible,

Or changing their shape to something not nearly so tempting,

If your lethal hatred was balked.

Only a woman treated thusly could share

Some of the anger, the despair, the hatred that you felt;

The need to strike out at the one who had hurt you so,

Or, failing that,

At the ones he had hurt you with.

When a woman has no such touchstone for the pain you felt,

It is easy to read the stories written by men,

And see you with clouded eyes,

Thinking you spiteful or cruel,

Instead of a woman seeking only the recompense of justice

For the crimes against you.

I understand you so much better now.

Hera, Delight of the World
by Rebecca Buchanan

The world delights to do You honor, Mighty Queen

At the sight of You

> mountains tremble

> lions bow

> birds sing in joy

The host of creation cries out in adoration

FARMER'S PRAYER TO HERA
by Rebecca Buchanan

Hera

Cow-Eyed

Watch over my herd

Keep them sure of foot

      strong and healthy

Keep their milk pure

      sweet and warm

HYMN TO HERA

by Frances Billinghurst

All hail Hera, O Regal One

Queen of the Sky and Starry Heavens

Daughter of Rhea, who was devoured by Kronos who rightly feared he would be usurped.

Was it Tethys and Oceanus who raised you once you were freed?

Or perhaps Temenus, son of Pelasgus?

Or even Asterion's daughters, later your nurses?

All hail Hera, O Exquisite One

Goddess of Women and Beauty

Did you not know the pet cuckoo you captured was your own brother disguised?

Your beauty enticed and seduced him, and so he seduced you,

And that was the first of his many betrayals.

Was your love only after your maidenhood?

They say you bathed daily in the Kanathos to recover that most sought after gem,

Yet still he wandered.

All hail Hera, O Devoted One

Goddess of most Sacred Vows.

What happened to the hieros gamos, said to last three hundred years, when you joined with your beloved in sacred union?

The place which Knossos, Samos, and even Mt Thornax vie to claim.

Of all heirs you gave him, he favoured those created without your sacred womb.

Did you weep at his indignities inflicted upon you?

Did you weep at his rejection of your offered intimacies?

All hail Hera, O Powerful One

Queen of all Gods

Matron Goddess of Argos and Samos

Although your beloved seeks not your wise counsel, nor shares with you his most intimate secrets,

It is you whom all heroes worship.

It was to you whom Gaia entrusted her sacred golden apples.

It is to you all doe-eyed lovers call, seeking your blessings from their tangled marriage beds.

O Regal One

O Exquisite One

O Devoted One

O Powerful One

All hail, Hera, all hail.

PRAISE HERA, GODDESS QUEEN
by Chelsea Luellon Bolton

I am Queen of Earth and Heaven, and of the Sea

All Nature belongs to Me

I am the tides and the wind and the lofty heights

These are My spaces where people worship Me at night

During the day, I am in My temples

and shrines in homes

I am honored, I am loved

I am the Goddess from Above

People look to the sky to see Me

for I am the starry sky

The wind blows when I say

The skies are Mine every day

The Gods above know Me as Queen

I rule over the home

Sovereignty and Nature are My domains

I am Goddess of the throne

I am the Wife of Zeus

That fickle God of Thunder

With all His paramours

They are His lovers and trysts

While I am His Wife

There are differences you see

between them and Me

I am the legal wife

The Queen of His Throne

No one has this honor, but Me

I am the Matriarch of His Home

His domain: the Sky

I am the Goddess of Rain and Stars

This domain is Mine

All Heaven is under My sway

In My duties I do not delay

Marriage, Childbirth

Goddess of them all

Women are My people

I am the Goddess of the Home

Women's duties are My own

Weaving, cleaning, raising children

Upkeep of the Home

I am also the Goddess of Virgins and the Young

For I am Parthenos as well

And Widow too

There is no part of a woman's life that I do not touch

Yes, even you

I am the Cow and the Peacock

For I am the Mother of All

The Glorious Goddess of Heaven

With Eyes that see

Nothing escapes Me

In Heaven and Earth

And Hades, as well

I am the All-Seeing Goddess

Of Heaven and Hell

For I am the Queen

Equal to My Husband

Both in Wisdom and Power

I am the Queen of Heaven

And He is the King

I am the Goddess of Showers

And I am equal to Him

He is equal to Me

Those that petition Him

May petition Me

For I am the Goddess of Land, Sky and Sea

I am the Queen of the Goddesses,

Queen of Gods

I am the fairest of All

Although Paris could not see

I would have given him sovereignty

He did not want this from Me

Herakles I honed

With trials and tests

And he became the greatest of men

Due to My interests

Leto's birth I did stop

Her labor pangs ceased

When the gods came to Me

Offering a boon

A necklace

I wanted

So I gave My assent

No time was spent

And as I stepped into the light

The sun was awfully bright

Leto have given birth

I knew of Their worth

Semele I tricked

into seeing Zeus

as I

In all His Godly glory

With flashing thunder of the Skies

She died of fright

I tricked her that night

And Her Babe

I did foreswear

I gave Him madness

And He produced the vine

and rites of frenzy

The Twice-Born God

Lover of wine

Hephaestus, My son

Whom I did betray

Banished when I saw Him

crippled, dismayed

Cast Him down

He came and made a throne for Me

Demanding Me to speak My Name

His Mother

Bound was I

in His bejeweled throne

until the Mad Wine God came

and made the Lame God drunk

And I was free

This ended the animosity between Him and Me

Kallisto, maid of Artemis

I did see

My Husband had lain with her

And that angered Me

The Maiden became a Bear

as My Power willed

Cast into the Heavens

As stars in the sky

Lady of Beasts I did persuade

To shoot her down that day

Echo did betray

When I came to her that day

She spoke so I would not see

the Nymphe running from Me

So then her punishment I gave

only she could speak when another bade

Her tongue made her a liar

And I made her a thief

The last few words

she can only speak

when another's voice

rings in her peak

They gave Gerana honors

She boasted

and did not see

why she should honor Me

A crane I made her

the ugliest bird

Who now dwells above her former herd

Beware of those who do not

give the Goddesses their due

I will not forgive you

Jason I did favor

As the Goddess from Afar

I aided him in his quest

To get the Golden Fleece

To overthrow the King

who would not honor Me

and killed a woman within My temple

I sent Hekate's Maid

to help him with her craft

Ancient Magic did she possess

In the end, Her heart had turned to wickedness

Ixion desired Me

and tried to take Me in his arms

My husband wished to have a test

Of this mortal's wretchedness

He formed a cloud

to look like Me

And see what that boy's fate would be

Ixion made a terrible boast

This was no joke

He told the Deathless Gods and Men

That I had slept with him

This was a lie

Now he would die

With cloud as shield

and ice in hand

I struck the Lady of Beasts on land

Her arrows shot at Me

I did not flee

My power and hail repelled

The swift arrows She expelled

At last the night was won

When I struck Her with a ton

I am the life of

Every Girl

Maiden,

Virgin,

Widow

and Wife

I am the Goddess of their life

I am Queen of Heaven, Earth and Sea

All belong to Me

I am wife of Zeus who left Him

Tired of His trysts

I gathered My might

and left Him that night

And He made a mock-wedding

to win Me back

I came and discovered His deceit

I wed Him then and every year

Forever, now I will always be near

I am the Goddess of Heaven and Hell

There is nothing I cannot dispel

A jealous wife, a jealous lover

A disturber of the Home

I do not allow this to go on

Where I dwell

I am the Goddess of the Home

This is My domain

Family as well

Blessings I disperse

Earn your worth

I am the Goddess Queen

Though People think I am mean

I test, I hone

Higher standards, have I

For I am the Goddess of the Skies

I am the White-Armed Goddess

Of the wind and sea

All raise their hands

All bow

All worship Me

I am the Goddess Queen

Queen of Gods, Queen of Men

My reign will never end

Hera's Plea to a Wicked God
by Christa A. Bergerson

I am the glorious heifer

yearning

for you to milk

my supple womb

Yet, you cast your seeds

elsewhere

The whores may lap up

your divine serum

but I shall drink it with fervor

Give me your flesh

it's all that I want or need

Leave your doubts at my feet

I will bleed you dry

but that is love, unabashedly

TRUTH ABOVE ALL
by Heather Kohser

Primordial Mother Hera whose body is earth

Were You raped by a Sky God in the guise of a cuckoo?

Cow-eyed Queen, Hera so beloved by Your people

Were you hung from the heavens -- still drenched with Your milk?

Is there nothing sacred?

I implore You -- Ancient Seer, Immortal Snake --

coiled transcendence crowned with wisdom

heal all who seek to know the truth!

Gift us with Your mystery, and mercy from the power of men --

who rule and write with their sex!

"HARMONY OF HERA AND APHRODITE"
by Lykeia

MYTHOS

FOOTPRINTS

by Rebecca Buchanan

Predawn light filled the interior of the tent, painting his boots and bullwhip and shotgun and sleeping bag and small backpack a soft red. Rubbing his eyes, Hank slowly sat up, grimacing at the pull in his lower right back.

The alarm on his iPhone wailed. He winced, reaching over to turn it off. Outside, a few of the cattle looed, startled by the sound, and Cyrus whined in response. The horse knickered. He really needed to get Cassie to change that; something less heart attack-inducing; like cannons, maybe.

He unzipped the sleeping bag and wiggled free, sliding down until he could easily reach his boots. His back twinged again. Grumbling, he pulled on his beaten up old combat boots, picked up used-but-almost-new at the Goodwill in Pensacola; the soles were still solid and the steel toes had saved him from a broken foot more than once, but he was going to have to reline them soon.

Stuffing his phone in his shirt pocket, he grabbed his backpack, bullwhip, and shotgun, and zipped open the tent. He took a deep breath of clean spring air, tinted with the scents of grass, pine, sea and cattle.

One of the beasties huffed, lifting her head as he emerged from the tent. With a delighted bark, Cyrus charged over, tail zipping back and forth. He buried his snout in Hank's hand.

"Mornin', boy." Hank scratched the dog's head and tugged at his ears. "Nothin' to report, I take it?" Hank looped the whip over a hook on his belt.

Cyrus barked, tilting his head, and several of the cattle mooed in response. Hank looked up, gaze critically passing

74

over the horse hobbled nearby and the small herd of cattle. Eight heifers, one bull, and one male yearling. The pineywoods breed in general were slim, graceful creatures with upward-curving horns and soft brown eyes, and his herd was no exception. The half-ton bull -- his hide brilliant white, his head a deep chocolate -- watched him for a moment, then went back to munching on wiregrass and the grass-like clumps that would one day grow into tall longleaf pine trees. The adult trees around them stood straight and thin, casting long sharp shadows in the early light. Somewhere nearby, a red-cockaded woodpecker was chiseling away at a pine tree, and a family of nuthatches were singing whee-hyah whee-hyah back and forth. A bobwhite quail interrupted the conversation.

Sighing, content for the moment, Hank lifted his hand from Cyrus and walked slowly over to the nearest heifer. She eyeballed him, chewing slowly. He gently pressed a hand to her swollen belly. Only a month to go, if that. He patted her side, then went to check on the other pregnant heifer; not quite as far along; maybe six weeks to go.

The bull whuffed proudly and tore up another mouthful of wiregrass.

"Yep," Hank agreed. "You did a good job, here." He yawned, then, and stretched, vertebrae popping. "Right, Cyrus, let's head -- "

He stopped, frowning down at the ground. His phone vibrated in his pocket. He crouched down, resting the butt of the shotgun against the ground, and examined the crushed wiregrass. Footprints? Bare footprints? Human? The phone vibrated again, impatient. Still studying the ground, he pulled it from his pocket and swiped his thumb across the screen. "Yeah?" he answered, distracted.

"Rise and shine, sleepyhead."

"Says the girl still wearing her jammies and bunny slippers."

"Hey," Cassie corrected him, "these jammies have skulls on them and the bunnies are zombies, thank you very much."

Hank grunted a laugh. "What happened to the little girl who liked fuzzy pajamas and cute, cuddly bunnies?"

"You were a bad parent and let me watch scary movies. Speaking of scary -- "

"Hmph."

" -- Clark Gideon of Gideon Gideon Thompson and Klein came by yesterday. Again."

Hank stood, frowning up at the rapidly lightening sky. The stark shadows of the longleaf pine trees softened and a flock of nuthatches pit-pit-pitted as they darted overhead. "Yeah? What'd he say?"

"The usual, but with another zero added."

Hank snorted. "Yeah? And what did you say?"

He heard the grin in her voice. "The usual, with a few four letter words added."

Hank shook his head, but couldn't help smiling himself. "My sweet little girl, all grown up. You're Mom would not be proud."

"The hell she wouldn't," Cassie giggled. A pause and her voice was sober when she spoke again. "The guy is serious, Dad. He's threatening to track you down and talk to you himself, instead of relying on me to relay messages." She paused again and a bit of humor had returned to her voice. "I guess he doesn't trust me to talk you around."

Hank frowned down at the footprints in the grass, then glanced over at Cyrus. The dog tilted his head up at Hank, one ear flopping over an eye. "He can try. I'll just file trespassing charges -- after I put some buckshot in his britches."

Cassie sighed. "Dad, as far as Gideon and his employers are concerned, the land is already theirs. Getting you to sign on the dotted line is just a minor inconvenience."

"Do you want me to sell?"

"Hell no," his daughter huffed. "I want you to keep it until I decide its valuable enough to kill you off so I can sell it then and go live in Belize. Or Mongolia. I haven't decided which yet."

Hank rolled his eyes. "All right. I'm moving the herd out to delta." Cassie and her silly codes. But, who knows ... Maybe Gideon did have the resources to tap their phones. "I'll talk to you tonight. Love you."

"Love you, too, Dad. Hug Cyrus for me."

"No," Hank averred, grinning, and clicked the iPhone off. A few minutes to tear down the tent, saddle up the horse, tie on his gear, and they were ready. "Okay, Cyrus, round 'em up." The dog barked excitedly, circling the herd. Stowing his shotgun in a side pocket, Hank pulled out his whip, cracking the tip. The cattle looed, shifted. The bull lifted his head and snorted. Another crack and the bull stepped forward, the rest of the herd falling into line, setting out into the morning.

***

Delta was a cool spot a few miles further inland, on the northern edge of Hank's property. The breeze still blew here, though it smelled less of sea and more strongly of pine. There were a few slash pines mixed in with the longleafs; galberries, huckleberries and blueberries sprang up in sunlit open patches. Lily, goldenrod, aster and violets dotted the ground. Hank chuckled as one of the heifers dove into a clump of the purple flowers, munching ecstatically. A flash in the corner of his eye, than another, faster: a wiry gray fox in hot pursuit of a cottontail rabbit. The whistle-trill of a tiny Bachman's sparrow. More flashes of color as a handful of painted buntings shot out of a galberry shrub and over his head. If Gideon and his ilk had their way, the whole forest would be ripped out to make room for a garish theme park. Or was it a mini-mall? Hank shrugged, and tilted his head back so he could see the trees framed against the bright blue sky of midday. Whatever it was Gideon wanted to build, he wasn't getting Hank's land to build it on. No way was he going to betray five generations of Overstreets, and all the generations to come, no matter how much money and how many court papers Gideon threw at him.

The bull snorted loudly, nudging one of the pregnant heifers.

"Don't worry, boy," Hank assured him, walking the horse closer. "I'm keeping a close eye on her and the young'un. You just keep doing your thing." He pulled out his canteen, taking a quick swig of cool water. "Make as many young'uns as you can, boy. Not many of you left." Another swig of water. "Not many of either of us left ...."

The herd spent a long afternoon grazing in and among the trees and shrubs. Occasionally the bull would bellow, and the yearling would answer, maybe a few of the heifers. A clump of sawtooth palmetto trembled when a cottontail rabbit dodged in and out of its den. Nuthatches whee-hyahed at him from high up in the branches, and somewhere a red-cockaded woodpecker drilled away.

As the sun slid down into the west, Hank hobbled the horse near a rich patch of wiregrass and flowers. He found a level spot nearby and had his tent up in a few minutes. He had just unrolled his sleeping bag when the phone in his pocket vibrated. He should have checked the screen before he answered it. "What's up, my girl?"

"Mr. Overstreet ...! So wonderful to speak with you again ...!"

Hank muttered impolitely under his breath.

"I'm sorry ...?"

"Nothing. How did you get this number, Gideon?"

"Now, now. Chuck, remember ...? Short for Charles ...?"

"Yep, unh-hunh." Hank pulled a pack of trail mix and an m.r.e. from his backpack. "Answer is still no."

"But you haven't heard my latest offer ...!"

"Don't wanna hear it. Cy Overstreet lost a leg running up San Juan Hill next to Teddy Roosevelt. Came home, bought a hundred acres of wilderness and a dozen head of cattle and settled down. We Overstreets have been here ever since, sweatin' and fightin' and dyin' if need be. He's buried here. So're his wife and his kids and their kids and everyone else, and my wife. We've been here five generations, we'll be here another five. I'm not about to let you bulldoze over them so you can build some superstore or mini-mall or parking lot or whatever the hell it is. Leave my daughter alone and do not call me again."

He clicked the phone off and slid it into his pocket. He rubbed at his forehead and then his lower back. Now he had a headache on top of his back ache.

Cyrus sidled up to him, sensing his mood. He pushed his nose against Hank's thigh, whining.

"Ah, no worries, boy. Come on. Let's eat and then hit the sack. Gotta move out again in the morning."

***

79

The klaxon alarm woke him. He jerked upright, tangled inside his sleeping bag. Ears ringing, it took him a few moments to dig his arm out of the bag and find the iPhone. Outside, Cyrus barked happily. Hank could just make out the dog's shape as he dodged in front of the tent and back around, spinning.

"It's all right, boy, settle down. I'll be right there."

But the dog continued to run in circles, round and round the tent and the horse and the herd. Hank frowned. The cattle were quiet, seemingly unconcerned. He crawled forward and yanked down the zipper. Cool morning air splashed across his face. He clambered out, boots in one hand, shotgun in the other. He spotted Cyrus off to his right, beyond the herd. Still frowning, Hank stepped around the bull and yearling and one of the heifers. They watched him with calm eyes, chewing thoughtfully. He stopped next to Cyrus, peering out into the early dawn. The forest slowly awakened around them, birds trilling.

Hank's voice was a near whisper. "What, boy?"

The dog barked again, but it was a happy, excited woof, not one of warning or fear.

Then he heard the sound behind him. A light whoof, a huff. A soft thud and whimper.

He turned, squinting. The bull stared at him for a moment, brown eyes serious, then slowly moved aside. Hank gaped. In the soft grass beside one of the heifers -- no, not a heifer anymore, but a cow -- lay a perfect milky white and earth brown calf. It twitched an ear in his direction and meeoooed. The calf's mother leaned over and licked its head, rough tongue a soft pink. Another twitch and the calf rose on shaky legs. One knee gave out, but the calf picked itself up again and slowly, slowly stepped in an awkward circle, head bobbing.

"Well ...," Hank breathed slowly. "Aren't you a surprise." He bent forward, peering at the calf. "An early surprise -- or was I that far off in -- " His words tumbled to a halt as he stared at the ground near the baby.

Footprints. Human. Barefoot.

He swung around, hand tightening on his shotgun again, and glared off into the forest. Cyrus continued to whine and bark, tail thumping excitedly. Nose wrinkled in anger, Hank eventually turned away from the trees and took a few slow steps towards the calf. The cow raised her head, snorted at him, and went back to licking her newborn. Slowly, Hank crouched down until he was eye level with the calf, then reached out a rough hand and gently touched its wet nose.

The calf sneezed and fell over.

Hank laughed. "Well, I'll be a son of a gun." He grinned, watching the calf clamber awkwardly back to its feet. He took a quick peek. "A boy, no less. Nice job." He nodded at the bull, who whiffed in response.

The calf stumbled forward and Hank's humor quickly faded at the sight of those barefoot tracks. Not Cassie. She would have let him know if she was coming out. He couldn't imagine Gideon running among the longleafs in anything other than thousand dollar loafers; actually, he couldn't imagine Gideon running among the trees at all unless it was to tag which ones he wanted torn down .... So, who else?

Cyrus trotted over, bumping his head under Hank's arm.

"Well, boy, looks like we've got a long night ahead of us."

***

81

The hoo-hoo-hoowha of a great horned owl. An almost human response from a couple of barred owls: who cooks for you, who cooks for you? Cicadas singing at the half moon. The distant howl of barking treefrogs and the quank-quank of the squirrel treefrog. Cyrus lifted his head, ears flat, when a choir of tiny chorus frogs started singing. Hank rested his hand on the dog's head; he could chase some of the little buggers later, after they figured out who --

Cyrus' head whipped around and his tail started slapping against the sleeping bag. Hank tightened his hand on the back of the dog's head and Cyrus stilled with a barely-perceptible whimper. Hank narrowed his eyes, peering out the open end of the tent. He watched as the bull raised his head and snorted. The new cow looked around, unconcerned, then went back to nursing her still-unsteady calf. The rest of the herd remained calm, quietly chewing or snoring.

He never heard her. Not a crunch of leaves or needles, not even a soft tread of foot over grass. She just slipped between the cattle, stepping lightly, almost dancing. Red dress of some kind of impossibly fine material gathered beneath full breasts. Hair the deep deep purple-black of midnight with twinkles of white -- stars? Milky white throat and arms and legs, exposed where she had tucked the hem of her gown into the band beneath her breasts. Laughter, as she danced among the cattle. She rested one hand on the bull's forehead for a brief moment, the animal bowing his massive head. Then on to the pregnant heifer and the yearling and the others, one after the other, bestowing a blessing upon each, until she got to the cow and calf. She knelt then, beautiful gown pooling in a crimson puddle around her legs, and placed a gentle kiss on the calf's head.

Hank's hand tightened on his shotgun. Cyrus whined, straining under his hand.

"You needn't concern yourself."

Her voice …. Hank swallowed hard. He wasn't even aware when Cyrus bolted out of the tent until he saw the dog at her side, tail waving wildly, bark ecstatic.

She laughed, a sweet-throated sound, rich like …. cherries dipped in chocolate. She put a finger to her lips and Cyrus stilled. Hank edged forward as she spoke again, her accent unplaceable, her voice calm but commanding. "I mean them no harm. They are safer with me than with anyone else -- even you. I offer them my blessing: long lives of green shaded grass, cool water, sweet milk, and many children." She turned her head then, and her smile stilled the whirling thoughts in his head, silenced his questions and accusations. "They understand, in their own way. They know they are few, and that you are trying to help them -- in your own way, for your own reasons." She tilted her head, motioning to him, and he found himself outside the tent, gaping at her stupidly.

"Own reasons," he repeated. He swallowed again. The lights in her hair …. "Yes, my family -- the cattle and land are all we have, are us, our life …. After the storm and the sickness and …." His voice trailed off.

"Only these few remained, the strongest and cleverest." She rose slowly, elegant, like one of those ballerinas in the old French paintings. Graceful, dignified. "They know you mean to kill them, once there are enough of them again, as you did before." She rested a hand on the side of the cow, petting it gently. The new mother whuffed and bent her head to tear up a mouthful of violets. "But they also understand that you care for them, that you respect them -- and that you give them the freedom of open sky and sweet wind and cold streams for the time they have, not darkness and cages and filth. For that, they are grateful." She turned her head towards him again and he realized, breath stopping, that her eyes were the same deep midnight as her hair and that the lights were stars, actual stars, twinkling and burning a thousand different shades of white and blue and red and yellow .... He jerked, startled, as she spoke. "As am I."

One last stroke of her hand along the calf's back. "Keep them strong, and they will keep you strong. Care for them, and they will care for you." She turned away, then, a queen dismissing her loyal subject. "I shall return, when they come into Cassandra's care."

She was red and milky white against the deep black and greenish-grey of the longleafs forest, stars bright in her hair. And then -- Cyrus barked -- gone.

It took a few moments for Hank to realize that he still had his whip in one hand and his shotgun in the other. He dropped them both, grimacing, feeling oddly ... ashamed. Cyrus ran over, sniffed at the weapons, then plunked his butt down in the grass and grinned up at Hank. One ear flopped over his left eye. "Well, boy, well, well, well, well." He sighed and rubbed a hand against his lower back. It took a moment for him to realize that it didn't hurt. He grinned. "Don't know what in the heck just happened or how I'm gonna explain it to Cassie, but dang I guess I better. Gotta warn her, after all, to expect the queen."

Author's Note: the Longleaf Pine Ecosystem, which once dominated the entire south-eastern United States, now occupies only a quarter of its former acreage. It is home to many rare, endangered, and unique flora and fauna, such as the red-cockaded woodpecker. Human population expansion, urbanization, commercial construction, the harvesting of trees for timber, and fire suppression (fire is critical to the regeneration and health of the longleaf) continue to threaten the ecosystem. Private institutions, state governments, and federal agencies are working to save the remaining forests.

Similarly, the pineywoods are an endangered breed of heritage cattle. The descendants of stock let loose in the wild by Spanish explorers, the breed evolved and adapted to the woody terrain of the southeastern United States and the Gulf Coast. Some herds were eventually redomesticated and became particular favorites of Florida ranchers, or crackers (so called for the sound of their whips). By the late 20th century, though, the breed had shrunk to only some two hundred animals on a few family farms in Alabama, Georgia and Mississippi.

WORDS FOR HERA
by Jack Wren

(Written for Use Within a Ritual)

I am Hera, called Bopis. I was and remain a Queen and a Goddess. I am the patron of marriage and birth, and even in my own realm I am disrespected. I am beautiful — beautiful enough to compete with Aphrodite, and that is no mean compliment. I am powerful. I had my own festivities celebrated at Argos. I am the firstborn daughter of Cronos and, yes, I am the wife of Zeus.

That's the only one people ever ask about these days.

Before the thunder came, I was a virgin goddess of the skies and stars, widely worshiped in Greece. My temples were some of the oldest and largest, and my statues once sat alone, regal and veiled. Zeus's image came later, after I let myself be seduced by the cuckoo. Remember that Zeus was often referred to as my consort.

You may remember also that the word cuckold comes from cuckoo.

He took my sky from me, my brother did, and my virginity. I gave it willingly, but I expected honestly and commitment in return. I am no Mary, no Queen of Heaven who was pleasantly chaste and happy to exist as a body surrounding a womb or a vehicle for a male god's pleasure. I am not someone to be trifled with. I won't let Zeus take any more from

me.

Say what you will about my treatment of Hercules, I gave him my own daughter Hebe in marriage when he came to Olympus finally. And you express such sympathy for Io, for

Danae, for Europa and for Leda, but you never seem to consider the context of this anger.

Perhaps it is unfair of me to expect humans and lesser goddesses to control themselves before a god such as Zeus. Perhaps they really are the simple things he seems to consider them, toys he can play with and then leave behind. But in my day, and in the days of Greece's glory, a

woman seduced outside of marriage — outside of my realm and without my blessing — was no better treated by her own family than she was by me. I doubt any of you would look any more kindly upon your husband's mistresses.

Let me ask you. If you were a powerful single goddess, one with the power to bring forth life — and children — from the earth without the help of a man, and you married a man who constantly ran off with the first cute human, or swan, or cow that passed by, would you be a

smiling Stepford Wife about it? I am the goddess who refused to be quiet. I am the wife who keeps the house no matter what, because it needs to be kept. I will not take my husband's shit, and I most certainly will not take yours.

Show me respect and a kind word, however, and I will be a pleased and pleasant Lady to keep your company. I am no more the bitch than any woman who has to be strong to maintain her place. Come sit by my hearth, and listen to my counsel, and I will teach you many things.

OF COERCION AND THE COSMOS

by Suzanne Thackston

"But why do you put up with it?' I asked. "You don't have to take that sort of treatment. You're so powerful and beautiful and wise. Don't be a victim! You know what you have to do, why don't you do it?"

She sighed. "You think you understand, but there are complexities in our relationship beyond your comprehension. The rules you play by are valid and correct for you, but they just don't apply to my marriage."

"Everybody says that!" I flung back heatedly. "Everyone thinks that their situation is unique and that no one understands. But I know what's right and what isn't. What about arete? You just can't be all squishy with bottom-line ethics. You have to take a stand!"

She smiled, brightening the candlelit room for an instant like a passing ray of sun. "That's one of the things I love about you. You're so passionate, all sizzling with righteous indignation, ready to change the world and save me. You're just so right."

"You're mocking me. I'm not a teenager. I'm a crone, and yeah, I've learned a few things along the way and one of them is when to haul out my sword and draw a line in the sand. Some things are not acceptable. Infidelity is not acceptable. Rape is not acceptable. Any form of violence is abhorrent in a consensual relationship. How can it be consensual otherwise?"

She was quiet for a few moments, dark lashes lowered, long fingers playing with a white jewel that dangled on a golden chain between her deep breasts. "Okay. Let me try and put this into terms that will make sense to you. Look into the fire, please."

We turned from each other on our couch and gazed into the smoldering flames of the banked fire. She whispered something I couldn't quite hear, the flames leapt up, roaring and crackling fiercely, then went abruptly dark, and I was Somewhere Else, watching as a woman hurried into a cluttered room ....

The tense look she threw over her shoulder was warranted when the man strode in after her. She whirled to face him, hands raised, palms forward in front of her, not defensively but in an attitude of warding. He paid no heed, reaching her in two long strides, big arms sliding possessively around her, pulling her hard into his body.

"No ..." she gasped. "Wait ...." But her voice was muffled by his lips at her throat. As his mouth came down on hers, her body melted into his for a moment, yielding longingly. Instantly he swept her up in his arms, his mouth never leaving hers, impatiently kicked aside a chair laden with boxes, sending it flying across the room. They fell together in a tangle of limbs onto the faded, lumpy couch.

But "Wait," she gasped again, turning her face away from him and trying fruitlessly to push him off. He laughed a little, breathlessly, his arms and legs capturing her and pinning her more securely underneath him.

"Listen to me!" she insisted. But he wasn't looking at her face; his eyes were intent on her body as he began to pull at her clothing, fingers rough with urgency. When he pulled back a little to free her blouse, she seized the opportunity, wriggling out from under him like a snake. She fell to the floor, but before he could grab her again she twisted to her feet and was across the room in an instant, putting the heaped dining room table between them.

He was on his feet and after her like a panther, breathing quickly, eyes aflame, his bare feet sliding on the worn throw rug. As she dodged around the table his brows snapped together.

"What the hell are you doing?"

She was panting, her hands fluttering in front of her. "You just -- you have to listen to me. Just -- wait. I need you to wait for me to say yes."

His jaw dropped. He stood stock still for an interminably long moment. There was honest bafflement in his eyes. "Wait -- for you to say yes to what?"

Her eyes pleaded with him. "You just grab me and go. Why can't you ever -- ask me? What if I don't want to?"

He let out an incredulous bark of laughter. "Don't want to? When the hell does that ever happen?"

"How would you know," she flared back. "You never bother to find out if I'm in the mood or not."

The brows came together again, slowly, ominously. "Mood? What does mood have to do with anything?" When she started to answer he cut her off with an impatient chopping gesture. "You hot little bitch. Don't pretend to be all virginal. You want it as badly as I do. Worse! Hell, woman, you half kill me sometimes."

"I know. I know. I'm not saying I want to stop. I'm saying that I want you stop railroading me. I mean, I should at least have the option to say no, shouldn't I?" She straightened, facing him squarely. "This is about respect. I love you and I know you love me. But you don't ever consider my feelings. It's all about what you want, when you want it."

Fury flashed electric blue in his eyes. Then it subsided. "So. You want me to -- what? Say please before we have sex? Where is this coming from?"

She sighed. "I don't know. I guess I just want some reciprocity. I want to feel as if I'm an equal in this partnership. To have a say."

His eyes narrowed, glinting. "Reciprocity. So, are you going to ask me pretty-please when you're wanting my ... services?"

Her chin went up. "If you like."

His laugh had an undertone of brutality. "So, now it's hearts and flowers, is it? Romance and roses? Long walks in the moonlight, and gazing into each other's eyes? We should start pretending that you're some simpering fluttery maiden, and I'm your preux chevalier? Listen, Lady. I deal in what is, and I know what we are. We don't need some adolescent illusion of courtship, and you can't refuse me any more than I can refuse you. When I want you, I must have you. And you don't want it any other way. Do you?"

Her eyes dropped, wavering, but then her jaw set. "I'm not suggesting some elaborate set of rules or that we play games. I just want to know that if I ever did -- if I ever do say no, that you will respect that."

Their eyes met, his hard, hers defiant. He said slowly, "Can you ever -- realistically -- think of an occasion where you would say no to me and mean it?" His gaze bored into her skull. "Be honest."

She looked at him. And looked at him. A small sound escaped her. "No."

Heat rose in his eyes. Abruptly he lunged towards her. In a second she had dodged behind the table, its box-strewn surface separating her from him. He looked at her incredulously. She was breathing hard, eyes brilliant, poised on her toes. His head lowered, a bull about to charge. Then he spun and stalked from the room. The door slammed.

91

She stood still for a moment, then let out a long, shaky breath. Her gaze softened, became pensive. Her teeth caught her soft lower lip, and she moved toward a dusty mirror. Humming, she ran her fingers through her hair, then deftly caught it up in a filet of purple wool, tendrils curling around her face. She looked thoughtfully at the door. She undid the top button of her blouse. She hurried out.

She turned back to me. "Do you see?"

I pondered. "I think I see more. But I still don't really get why there can't be -- I dunno -- more softness. More give. Why is it so wrong to strive for equality?"

She was silent for a moment. Then she gestured with a graceful white arm, and I found myself Somewhere Else, watching a tsunami. The water sucked back, retreating impossibly, unfathomably away from the shore. My mouth gaped as the wall of water rose, and rose, rushing toward me faster than horses can gallop, terrifying and unstoppable. It smashed into the land, kept rolling, broke apart, and now all I could see was water, and devastation.

I heard her voice, soft by my ear. "Did the Dark-Maned One ask politely? Did the rolling fields by the shore consider, and then give permission?"

A volcano erupted before us, spewing lava and ash high into the sky. Forest and field were choked for miles and miles around. Not one living thing remained.

"Is that consensual?"

A galaxy unfolded before my dazzled eyes, with darkness at its heart. Stars whirled around it, an immense and stately dance, stretched, streaked and fled into the chasm.

"Think, little one. What are you watching? Whom do you see? Is there a victim?"

I was silent a while, colors with no names pouring across my face. Finally I said, unable to look away, "I won't call you 'misunderstood' any more."

A beautiful forefinger brushed my cheek. "Your human customs," she mused. "How we love you for them. It's so unique, this fierce, quixotic, misguided quest for 'equality.' Outside your little reality there is balance, but 'fairness' just isn't a factor. And yet how magnificent you are as a species for pushing yourselves to foist it upon each other. What you keep forgetting, though, is that your rules and conventions don't apply to us. Gnothi seauton, dearest. It's not a warning, or a threat, or even an admonition. It's just a statement of Truth."

I looked up at her. "But are you happy?"

Her fingers slid along my face, cupping my chin. "You are a good child, little crone," she said. "I approve of your frantic flailing for understanding. I am, after all, Binah to his Chokmah."

The wide dark eyes held mine. And then she smiled. I was transfixed. I stopped breathing. I think my heart may have stopped beating. When I returned to myself I was alone. There remained only the lingering scent of apples, and a single peacock feather.

THE REBIRTH OF STACEY CARPENTER
by Jason Ross Inczauskis

Author's Note: The following is a work of fiction. Any resemblance to other persons or events, real or imaginary, is purely coincidental. In the event that this coincidence occurs and you find it unpleasing, please accept my apologies and know that it was unwitting, and that I intended no harm.

I have always had a deep fascination with the world of dreams. Ever since I was a young boy, I have sought to learn ever more of that chaotic nocturnal dimension that we all journey to when our eyes close in slumber. I never troubled my parents about trying to stay up late, so anxious was I to undertake my next exciting journey. Even while awake, my mind constantly moved from one thing to another, possessed of a wanderlust that could only be satisfied by unending flights of fancy. It became my life's work, much to my parents' chagrin. Perhaps that would not have been the case, if I had only focused my waking attention on becoming a proper psychologist. Such was not to be, though, as my wandering thoughts could never be bothered to focus upon my schoolwork, and my grades suffered greatly for it.

This is not to say that I lacked intelligence, no matter what my teachers may have said amongst themselves or to my parents. It was purely a lack of attention which hobbled my academic progress, which ultimately proved to be present only for those subjects that society felt was important for every child to be taught. Left to my own devices, I was quite capable of finding things that could herd my meandering thoughts, and I spent countless hours lost happily in the worlds crafted by Bradbury, Lewis, Verne, and Tolkien, amongst many others. In fact, I might even suggest that it was the effective dreaming of Ursula K. Le Guin's protagonist in The Lathe of Heaven that first led me to believe in the ability of dreams to change our lives. Though the worlds born from the dreams of George Orr may not have turned out for the best, I was confident that in an individual, changes could be made that would render that individual a better, happier person.

That was why I embraced dream interpretation early on in my career. I believed that if a person could understand what it was that a dream was trying to tell them, they could bring these lessons out into the real world. I began to write books of my own on that very subject, and traveled the country giving lectures and autographs out of the bookstores that carried my work. It was usually the stores specializing in New Age books that had the largest turnouts for my lectures, and it was at one of these that I first encountered Stacey Carpenter, a most remarkable woman.

I had been there to promote my newest book, Lucid Dreaming Day to Day: Change Your Dreams, Change Your Life. Like I always do at these functions, I had the available chairs pulled into a circle so that we could all have a discussion together. This is generally my favorite part of my book signings, as I get to vicariously enjoy the dreams of people I am meeting for the first time. Although many of them may be simple wish fulfillment for the dreamer, every now and then I hear one that stands out as especially meaningful. Ms. Carpenter's was just such a dream.

At this particular signing, there was a fairly large crowd for the small space available in the back room of the shop, numbering at least twenty. The patrons of the New Age shops often have some of the more interesting stories to share, perhaps owing to their greater acceptance of the potential meaning inherent to their dreams. Sadly, I also see a lot of self-aggrandizement at these events, and I have more than once witnessed a person claim that his or her dreams were communications from whichever form they personally attributed to the Divine, or from malicious entities actively working against said form of the Divine. I try not to pass judgment on such things, but it is difficult to believe claims from a person who obviously believes or wants others to believe that they have great significance far surpassing that of any other in the eyes of the Divine. Far be it from me to begrudge anyone their flights of fancy, but I think that all such claims should be taken with a large grain of salt.

That said, dreams that are believed to come from a heavenly source are not at all uncommon, and so long as the person seems to be benefitting from it rather than using such dreams as a way to obtain followers or stroke their own ego, I see no real harm in them. When Stacey Carpenter began her story, I initially feared it would be one of the latter. She clearly believed that her dream stemmed from a Divine source, in this case, the Greek Goddess called Hera. This was a potential red flag, as sometimes those that claim a Divine source for their dreams follow it with reasons why everyone else should accept their dream as reality and follow the course of action that they dictate. She also claimed that this dream of hers had saved at least three lives, which was another red flag, as claims such as these are often either lies to impress others or outright delusions of the individual. Suffice to say, when she began her story, I had little hope for her.

As she told her story, though, I realized that I had perhaps been hasty in judging her. She differed from many others who had made claims to dream communications with the Divine, in that she did not seem to think that she had been chosen for any special destiny. This became clear as her story went on. She also made no attempt at convincing everyone else that they should follow her or look upon her as a holy person. Instead, she believed that she had been given this dream to drive her towards getting the help that she desperately needed. As she later told me: "That dream wasn't a call to some sacred destiny. It was a call to grow up and think for myself. But now that I think about it, maybe those two things aren't so different."

Did her dream come from the Goddess Hera, as she claimed? I can't say. Maybe they do have a Divine origin. Maybe it was just the subconscious thoughts of Ms. Carpenter helping to stabilize her during a difficult and trying time. Regardless of the source, the effect that those dreams had on Ms. Carpenter is nothing less than extraordinary. I see it as excellent support for my theory that dreams can allow us to change our lives for the better. I am including the transcript of Ms. Carpenter's dream here with her permission.

***

Hi, everyone. Umm … Sorry, I'm a bit nervous. Where to begin … Well, my name is Stacey Carpenter. Ummm … Many of you may already know me from my work at the daycare, or from my time as High Priestess of the Campus Pagan Alliance that my husband … Sorry, my ex-husband, Darian Young, founded at the school. I see some familiar faces, so that's good. I hope that those of you remember do so kindly, and I hope that you will continue to do so even after you hear my story, though I don't much expect that. I know that if I were in your chairs and hadn't experienced what I had, I'd find it to be pretty difficult. This story is about how the great Goddess Hera gave me guidance when I needed it the most.

Anyway, my marriage was not as good of one as you might expect. I know, I know, this isn't part of the dream, but the dream kind of needs the circumstances to frame it properly, so please bear with me. As I was saying, I looked a lot happier about it in public than I was at home. It's not that it was all bad. I mean, we had our good times, and our bad times. We had our daughter, Lauren, and that was one of the best things. For her alone, my suffering was worth it. With any luck, I can expect some grandkids in the next few years. She's seeing this guy, Jake …. Sorry, I kind of went off on a tangent there. Please forgive me. The point I was trying to get across was that the whole thing was a mixed blessing, but if you don't count our daughter, on the whole it was more bad than good.

I met Darian during my last year of school. He had been teaching for a few years at this point, and no, he wasn't one of my professors. I met him when he was trying to start up the Campus Pagan Alliance. Back then, there wasn't a whole lot of us, and it was a bit of an uphill battle trying to get anything established. Darian was stubborn, though, and he didn't give up for anything. When we first started meeting, there was only five of us, and we were down to four by the end of that first year. Of course, by that point, I was completely enamored of him. He was young. He was handsome. He had interesting views. More importantly, he seemed to like me back. When that first year ended, instead of going away to try and get a career for myself, I moved in with him, and soon we were married.

Well, I soon learned the error of my ways. He was young, and handsome, and had interesting views, just as I'd noticed, but what I hadn't noticed was that he was also a sexist ass. He expected me to obey him in everything, no matter what. It started out as little things, so I just let it slide at first. Eventually, though, he was pretty much controlling my whole life. I wasn't allowed to get a career for myself or even hold down a job. At first he let me babysit, but eventually he forbade even that. After a couple years, he decided that the Campus Pagan Alliance now had enough people in it to require an expanded leadership council, which would take its flavor from the Olympian Gods. Each person in a 'leadership' role, and I use the term loosely, would be expected to perform certain functions. Guess whose role was Zeus?

Well, since Darian was Zeus, I was put in the Hera role by default. At the time, I didn't even know that much about the Greek Gods, though I did start reading some of the myths at that point to better understand. As the High Priest, every other member of the group was expected to follow his orders. As High Priestess, my only jobs were to help facilitate rituals and do his bidding. He never let me forget that, either. He wasn't just my husband, but my king at that point. He expected to be treated that way. He even struck me a couple times for talking back to him … At home, not in public. Never in public. It was the worst when he drank. I'm lucky, though, in that he always focused his anger on me. Never on Lauren. It might not be much, but I'd rather suffer abuse than see my daughter do so.

He began cheating on me, too. That hurt more than I would have cared to admit. I suffered what he dished out, but he wanted more than just his doormat. Now that I was the mother to his child, he felt he needed to go out for the occasional tryst with a drunken coed rather than coming to our bed. He didn't do it often that I knew about, but when I called him on it, he would strike me. I had no right to question him, is what he'd say. He was the king, and if he wished for another lover, he would take one whether I liked it or not. After all, if Zeus could take another lover, why couldn't Zeus's greatest follower do the same? I was just the wife, and had no say in the matter. He even had the nerve to say that faithfulness was my job alone, since I was a follower of Hera.

Once Lauren went away to college, I started to become a little bolder. I was no longer worried that he might take out his frustrations on her instead of me, and he had succeeded in instilling an unhealthy opinion of my own worthlessness, so I no longer cared quite so much about what happened to me. The last straw, though, was a young woman by the name of Ashley Dayton. Ashley was a pretty blonde graduate student in his lab. The same age as our daughter. The same damn age! I can't say I was truly surprised that he was fu … Ummm … Sleeping with her. I knew the warning signs. More 'late nights at work'. Why he even bothered to lie to me about it was beyond me, since he'd already made it perfectly clear that he didn't give a rat's ass what I thought about anything.

One night, he came home. He had alcohol on his breath, and seemed to be in a surprisingly good mood. It didn't look like it would be good for me, though. He told me, in no uncertain terms, that our time together was done. He didn't love me anymore. He was divorcing me so that he could marry Ashley after she graduated. He said that a man like himself deserved a sexy young wife, not the tired old thing I'd become. He'd drawn up some papers that he wanted me to sign, too. Papers that said that I was giving him everything and that I wouldn't seek alimony or anything like that. He expected me to sign the papers, and walk out that night with nothing but the clothes on my back. I refused. Leaving me for another woman was bad enough, but for him to have the audacity to try and kick me out of my home and tell me to basically go die in a ditch somewhere? Fuck that! Sorry, I didn't mean to say that. It just kind of slipped out.

So ... Umm ... Anyway ... So, I refused to give him what he wanted. I told him that if he was going to treat me like that, that I was going to take him for everything I could. Then he gave me the worst beating of my life. When he stormed out that night, he told me that I'd damn well better sign those papers, or he'd give me a worse beating than that. I knew what I had to do, though. Darian had insisted a few years ago on getting a handgun for personal protection. He then promptly put it into the back of the closet and forgot about it. I hadn't, though. I'd thought about that gun a hundred times in the few years we'd had it. I had thought about getting it out and using it, either on him or myself. It never went beyond that, though, until that night.

That night, I pulled it out, and carefully loaded it. I'd never shot it before, but I figured that if I was close enough to him, I wouldn't be able to miss. I drove around all night looking for him, but never actually found him. I did tear up the papers, though, so he couldn't forge my signature on them. He'd done things like that before. It hadn't occurred to me at the time that he could simply get more papers and do the same thing, though in the end he didn't, so I guess it doesn't matter. I didn't sleep, though. Instead, I staked out the university and waited for him to leave, then followed him to find out where it was that he was staying. The girl was living in a small duplex just off campus. I drove home to wait until nightfall, then went back.

I parked about two blocks away, then snuck towards the little house. I saw Ashley carrying in a couple cases of soda, closing the door behind her. Darian's car was still parked out front. I was planning on going in through the front door if it wasn't locked and killing them both, followed by myself. Then Darian's folks arrived. I mentally cursed. As much as I hated Darian, I had nothing against his folks, and I didn't want to kill them or force them to watch me kill him, so I realized that I wasn't going to be able to do it that night after all. That's when I went home.

I dropped to my knees in front of my Hera altar. There wasn't much there. A candle, an offering dish, and a statue of the Goddess with a peacock. I didn't even have a peacock feather there anymore. I looked at her, and I began to cry. I'm not sure what I said in those moments. I don't remember them very clearly. I fell asleep eventually, though, right there in front of the altar.

When I opened my eyes, I was beside a great stone fountain gushing water up towards the sky. The horizon was still bright with the colors of sunset, but the sky above was jeweled with stars. Despite this, a shimmery rainbow danced among the jets of water. Looking around, I saw numerous buildings that were obviously of ancient Greek construction, though they were brightly colored rather than white like we usually think of them. The fountain I was near was also pretty high up in the mountains, giving me an amazing view.

"It's quite lovely, isn't it?" a male voice asked from directly beside me.

I almost jumped out of my skin, then turned to see the peacock who had silently slipped up beside me. "Umm ... yes, it is quite lovely. You can talk."

101

"Ah, how perceptive of you. That would slip right by most people, but you noticed." I didn't quite know how to respond to the peacock that seemed to be mocking me, but the bird continued on without waiting for me to do so. "Queen Hera has sent me to fetch you to her. Follow me."

The bird turned and strutted away, and I followed, having no reason not to do so. He led me into a great palace, and the beauty inside was just as beautiful as the beauty outside had been. I'm not sure I could do justice to it with words, but I'll try. Each of the pillars was beautifully carved in a different image, and gold and jewels covered everything. Here and there were peacock feathers inlaid into the stones made from gemstones. When I was led into the throne room, Hera's throne seemed to be crafted from more of these jeweled feathers.

If I was surprised by my surroundings, though, my hostess was even more impressive. I had always pictured Hera as a matronly middle-aged woman with a perpetual scowl or a cold look of neutrality upon her face. The Hera that greeted me here was nothing of the sort. She seemed a beautiful woman in the full blush of youth, though her brilliant eyes seemed to hold the wisdom and experience of ages within them. Her raven black hair shimmered with the purples, blues, and greens of the peacock feathers with which she surrounded herself. Her expression was not one of imperious wrath or disdain, but one of boundless joy and love.

"Welcome, Stacey," she said to me, great warmth filling her voice. "I trust that you have enjoyed yourself so far?"

"Of course," I said, dropping to my knees and bowing my head. "Everything is so beautiful here. Thank you for allowing me to gaze upon your home."

"There's no need for that," she said, laughing. "I didn't bring you here to bow down before me. I brought you here because you needed help."

I raised my eyes to look upon her once more. "You're going to help me?"

"Truly a wise one, this," the peacock said. "Very quick on the uptake."

"Hush, you," Hera said playfully to the peacock. "There's no cause for such rudeness. Yes, Stacey, I am here because you need help."

I found myself breaking into a wicked grin. "That's wonderful. We can kill the bastard together. Can you believe what he pulled?"

Hera laughed. "I can. I am not generally surprised by the selfish and shortsighted actions of any person. But no, I'm not going to help you kill him."

"Then how is it that you're going to help me? Aren't you enraged by what he did? ...Oh, it's because he's a follower of Zeus, isn't it? You don't want to make Zeus mad."

Hera laughed again. "First, I'm not concerned with making my husband mad. It's not as easy to do as one might think. Second, Darian is not a follower of Zeus."

I frowned. "But ... but he's based his whole life around being like Zeus."

"He is nothing like Zeus," Hera said. "Do I strike you as the type to bind myself in marriage to someone like that? Of course not! Zeus is a great and noble being, like all the Gods. What your husband has done is not decided to emulate Zeus, but rather to use popular depictions of Zeus as an excuse for indulging in the behavior he wishes to indulge in. You see it all the time. Alcoholics that call themselves followers of Dionysos. Men and women who cheat on their spouses calling themselves devotees of Aphrodite. Barroom brawlers who insist that every punch they throw is done in the name of Ares. Look around the world, and you'll never find a shortage of men and women who

103

eagerly indulge their vices and try to creatively proclaim themselves holy for doing so."

"That seems so wrong ...," I began to say.

"Of course it's wrong," she replied. "People interpret the stories too literally. They depict the Gods as selfish children! Children who kill someone or sleep with them at the drop of a hat. That's not really the way it works. Those events are symbolic."

"So you're not jealous of Zeus and his many lovers, then, because Zeus doesn't have many lovers?"

"Yes and no," she said. "I am not jealous. We Gods are not the jealous sort. Zeus has many interactions with mortals that could symbolically be represented as taking them as lovers, but he does not go down and engage in sexual relations with them. Likewise, when you see me in myths putting challenges before the heroes, I am not their enemy."

"You're not?"

"No. That, too, is something that people misunderstand. I am helping to push them onwards. Drawing them towards the Gods. I see the beauty in their souls, and I try to help them develop that beauty, making them ever more godlike. I am not one who hates the hero, but rather, one who loves them greatly."

"Why do you allow people to depict you as the villain so often, then? Why don't you tell them what you've told me, and make them show you the respect you deserve?"

"It is not my place to interfere with the free will of mankind. If they wish to portray us in a negative light, that is their choice. It doesn't change the truth of things. A God does not become a lowly individual because people depict them as such. Nor does a woman become worthless because her husband treats her as such."

"I know that," I began to say. "But ...."

"But you act as though that is the case. When he told you that you had to submit to him, that you were the inferior one in the marriage, you accepted it. If anything, you should have ended this marriage a long time ago."

I guess I was a little surprised. "Ended the marriage? But, I thought you wanted people to stick to their marriages ...."

"Marriage is a delightful institution, so long as it is healthy for all involved. I am not just a Goddess of marriage, though. That's another one of those popular depictions that results in the Gods being depicted as less than they are. We are not archetypes. We are living beings. Any depictions of us are just that. We are no more the way we are depicted than you are a photograph of yourself. The only way to know who you really are is to be yourself, and not let the depictions of others shape you into something that you are not."

"So what should I do?" I asked softly.

"Live your life," she replied. "Get a divorce. On your terms, not his. Don't let bitterness and jealousy consume you. Don't let your anger blind you to the consequences of your actions. Seek help from many sources. Not help with murder. That's not what you really want. You want support. Talk to your daughter. Talk to a therapist. Talk to me. Judge for yourself. You are your own person. Act like it. The best revenge you can possibly have is to deny him the satisfaction of your misery."

I thought about that for a minute. "You're right. I will do so. I will be the best person I can be."

"That's all we ask," Hera said with a smile, leading me by the hand back outside. By this point, the sun was beginning to rise, casting its light over the mountains and valleys. The fountain's rainbow came alive in the early morning light, sparkles of blinding white light dancing around it.

"Thank you so much," I said. "Olympos is even more beautiful than I dreamed."

At that, both Hera and the peacock began to laugh. "Is that where you think you are?" she asked.

"Well, yes," I said. "You mean I'm not?"

"No, dear Stacey," she said. "This is my home, certainly, but it is the home that you built for me within yourself. All this beauty is within you. Show it to the world."

I snapped awake on the floor in front of my Hera altar. It was morning now, and the gun rested on the floor beside me. I didn't want to use it anymore, though. The first thing I did that morning was find a shop that would purchase firearms and sell the thing to it. I figured it would be best to get rid of it before I began to think about using it again.

When I got home, I called my daughter, and told her everything that had happened. The night before, I mean. I was still coming to terms with the dream. Lauren was pretty upset that Darian had tried that, but she promised that she'd get me the help I needed. It turned out that Jake's father was a divorce attorney, and a pretty good one, and he agreed to represent me in the trial. Suffice to say, the divorce trial didn't work out as well for Darian as he'd been hoping. I don't expect the alimony to last very long, though. It seems that somebody reported his inappropriate relationship with a student, and now he's in danger of losing his job.

You know, he actually tried to get me back? Ashley dumped his sorry ass the second she graduated. He said he was sorry. He said that he missed me. He said that he could change. I told him that I already had, and no longer needed him. I felt so alive that day! I try not to take joy in the misfortunes of others, but it's hard not to where he's concerned.

He's out of my life, now, I'm proud to say. After what he pulled, Lauren has decided that she's not going to invite him to her wedding. She doesn't want him to end up ruining the day by trying to reassert control over me. Not that I'd let him. That period of my life is done. I'm my own person, and I won't let anyone else take that from me. I feel reborn.

Don't get me wrong. This isn't a 'happily ever after' here. I still struggle with low self esteem, and the bitterness isn't completely gone. Sometimes, I even fantasize about what it would have been like if I had gone through with it. I know, it's terrible, but I still do it. But that dream was an excellent source of motivation. I've been seeing a therapist for the last two years, now, and I think that Dr. Franks is really helping me. I still have my issues, but I'm coming to terms with them. It helps now that I'm working, and have something to occupy my mind. Something productive, where I feel like I'm making a difference. It will probably be years before I no longer need therapy, if there ever comes a time when I don't at all. I don't mind, though. I'm just doing what I need to.

I've also listened to Hera's advice. I try to live the best way that I can. I try to push my inner beauty out into the world whenever I find the opportunity. Whenever things get tough, I call Lauren or Dr. Franks and tell them what's on my mind. Sometimes, it's just good to have someone to listen. They have both been very supportive of me. I also talk to Hera every morning, and I know that she's always listening. I know I'm no hero, but I still feel like she's pulling me towards the Gods. And, it may sound strange, but every time I find myself questioning everything or needing to call someone for support, I feel like I can feel her smiling upon me, and that everything will work out for the best in the end."

SELECTIVE MEMORY

by Gerri Leen

Mnemosyne lay in the meadow grass, listening to her daughters' laughter. Nine muses, their voices raised in song, free from care. Except for Melpomene. But she could even make tragedy a sweet thing.

Mnemosyne remembered tragedies that weren't even hers. And they were never sweet.

She noticed a peacock strutting down the far side of the meadow, felt dismay come over her. Not now. Not today.

The bird let out a harsh cry.

She saw Clio running across the grass; her daughter waved to her.

The bird cried again, the sound impatient.

Mnemosyne got up and walked to the peacock.

Its voice was no prettier than its cry. "My mistress needs your assistance."

"Why today?" The sun was so bright, the wind sweetly cool.

"She is waiting."

"Fine." She could not ignore the call: she was only a Titan, and Hera was the queen of the gods.

The peacock spread his tail, and the sunlit meadow gave way to a shadowed, misty realm. Hera stood between two rivers, wrapped in a white cloak edged with gold.

Mnemosyne walked to her river -- the river of memory -- rolling by stormy and dark. Lethe's river of forgetfulness

108

meandered gently on her other side, light from some unknown source dappling it.

Hera looked up, assessing Mnemosyne. "I need your help."

"I know. This is about him?" Him: Zeus. Mnemosyne's lover before he married this beauty who could not hold him.

Hera met her eyes, holding her hands out in a helpless gesture. "I've forgotten things. He told me I have. I must have drunk from Lethe."

"If you've forgotten anything, it might have been on your own. The mind can do that. To protect us."

"I'm a god. We don't just forget." Hera knelt down by Mnemosyne's river, cupping her hands to hold the water.

"Why do you need me here? If you wish to drink, do so." She knew how this would go, wanted to be somewhere else.

Hera drank. Her expression did not change; she seemed to be waiting for something. Then she laughed -- a forced expulsion of air rather than sound. It sounded almost ... helpless. "I can't remember."

Mnemosyne moved closer, sinking to the ground next to Hera, feeling the cool mist rise up around her. "If it is in you to remember, my river would have found the memory."

"It was part of me, once. Zeus told me it was."

"What is it you wish to remember?" But she knew. This was part of the game.

"I want to remember what it was like to love him without the anger I feel now. Without the pain of betrayal."

"Perhaps you have never loved him the way you want to remember?"

"Perhaps not. I remember only this pain. It hurts worse now than it did before I drank."

Hera's eyes blazed, and a fierce wind came up, blowing water from Mnemosyne's river in great sheets. But Hera could not stop it from flowing, could not do more than momentarily lower the level. Memory would not be denied.

Lethe's river began to bubble behind them, and Lethe appeared on the bank, smiling the sinister smile of her mother Eris. "The only way to love a man like Zeus is to start fresh." She held out a goblet that shone with the same strange light of Lethe's river.

Hera eyed the offered gift. She seemed to be remembering something. "I've done this before. I've been here before."

Mnemosyne looked down. Hera had been here before. Many times. And each time she called her to witness.

"You knew." Hera stared at her, lovely brown eyes accusing Mnemosyne of betrayals she had never committed.

"I always know."

"You never hated him, did you? You only loved him? You gave him such beautiful children." Hera sounded like the little girl she'd never been allowed to be.

Mnemosyne felt her heart go out to her. Wanted to hold her, to comfort her. But Hera would not want that. Right now, she wanted only the truth.

"I never hated him." But Mnemosyne's love had been fleeting. She'd been blessed in that.

"Here. Drink." Lethe leaned over, the goblet finding its way into Hera's grasp.

For a moment, Mnemosyne thought Hera might not drink, but then she lifted the goblet to her lips. Her face went slack, held the innocence of a child, the expectation of a young woman. Hera blinked and looked around, as if surprised to find herself in Persephone's realm. "Where is Zeus?"

There was a flash of thunder, and he appeared, his beard freshly combed, his breath sweet with mint. "My love."

Hera ran to him, and he wrapped her in a thundercloud and carried her out of the underworld.

"Why?" Mnemosyne had wondered it before, but she'd never asked. She knew why Zeus wanted it but didn't know why Lethe helped.

"Even discord gets old," she heard Eris whisper, her disembodied voice causing a chill down Mnemosyne's spine. "But to see it start afresh, to feel it take hold -- that is a gift I cannot enjoy without my daughter's help."

Lethe sighed. "Someday, I will defy you, mother. I will take away all her memories so she won't remember loving him at all. She'll finally be free."

"You say that every time," Mnemosyne said. The weight of Lethe's forgotten words settled onto her before they tumbled into her river.

"Do I?" Lethe asked, as she sank back into her own river, a slave to it. But a peaceful one.

Mnemosyne heard Eris's harsh laughter echoing through the mist and wished herself back to the meadow. The sun shone brightly, taking away the chill from Hades. The peacock was gone, and she saw a gold-tipped cloud that rumbled with thunder.

111

Hera was getting to know her husband again.

"Mother?" Euterpe ran to her, humming a merry tune as she took her hands. "Come sing with us. Do you remember the song Hermes taught us?"

Mnemosyne nodded. There was nothing she could not remember.

Even if she'd rather forget.

The wind blew, and Hera stood on the summit of Mount Olympus, looking for Zeus. Far in the distance, she saw a thundercloud, lightning flying across it. Closing her eyes, she concentrated and heard the sound of tinkling laughter and her husband's hearty cries of pleasure.

"Mother?" Hebe's sweet voice sounded from behind her.

"Go away. I want to be alone."

Hebe came to stand next to her and stared out at the cloud. "It's his nature to stray."

"It shouldn't be. Not when we love each other."

"Why do you always act as if it's the first time when he does this so often?"

Hera stared at her. When had Zeus ever done this to her?

Hebe's eyes were full of pity. "Come, let's take your chariot out."

Hera tried to ignore the hurt inside her. She was the Queen of the Gods. She would not cry. "I want to get far away from here."

Hebe led her to the stables, hooked the horses to the gold and silver chariot. Hera stepped onto it, and the horses

112

pranced nervously, then Hebe jumped in beside her, and they were off. They hit the lowlands, and Hera slashed the reins, sending the horses in the opposite direction from where Zeus hid in the clouds.

The forest gave way to scrub, the green turning to tan. Hera stopped the chariot at a crossroads, felt a familiar shudder take her as she entered Hecate's realm.

Hebe seemed to shrink in on herself, her normal vivacity squelched in this dying land. "I don't like it here."

Hera handed the reins to her daughter and jumped off the chariot, landing with a puff of dust, scattering scorpions and serpents.

"You." Hecate sat on a rock, her weathered skin, tan robe, and dun-brown hair blending into the desert. She rose, the trailing hem of her robe leaving a current of dust in her wake. "You don't tend to frequent the crossroads unless you want something."

Hera tried to remember if she'd been here before? She had no recollection of coming to this place, but something in her memories felt incomplete.

Hecate pressed her hand against Hera's forehead, then dropped it hastily and gave Hera a look full of disgust .. and pity. "What we do to ourselves for love."

"I don't understand."

"No," Hecate said, walking away. "I know you don't."

"I did not give you leave." But as she said it, Hera had to suppress another shudder. She might be the Queen of the Gods, but Hecate was something else -- something older.

"Mother, come away." Hebe frowned, her young beauty shining like a white flower in the desert.

Hera knew she'd once been as fresh as Hebe, before she'd born children to Zeus, before her hips had grown rounded and her breasts full and heavy. She glanced at Hecate, thought she saw three faces where there had been one before. A crone, a young girl, and a woman such as herself, ripe with possibility.

"Why do you give away all that you are?" Hecate clapped her hands, and a line of scorpions and spiders followed her as she walked away.

"What did she mean?" Hebe asked as she took Hera's hand to guide her into the chariot.

"I don't know. But I know who will." Hera took the reins, leaned toward the horses, and whispered, "Mnemosyne."

They raced back over the desert, onto land that grew green and lush. Mnemosyne was alone, lying in a meadow watching the birds fly overhead, turning slowly to watch Hera drive up. She stood, staring at Hera in what looked like surprise. "My queen."

Hera left Hebe in the chariot and crossed her arms to keep warm in a breeze gone suddenly chill. "I have forgotten something."

"Yes?" Mnemosyne looked nervous.

"I'm sure of it. Just as I think I've been here before."

"Here? In this field?"

"Here. At this moment of choice."

Mnemosyne sighed. Then she nodded.

"Take me to your river."

"Hera, I --"

"Take me to your river. At once."

114

They were suddenly there, standing in a place between two rivers. Lethe's waters of forgetfulness, so clear and sweet looking. And Mnemosyne's river of remembering, the water stormy with lost truths.

Hera did not hesitate. She knelt and drank.

The truth hurt. It stung like the barbs of a million tiny bees attacking her heart. Memories flooded her, and she slammed her hand down on the water, causing a huge surge to wash over her and Mnemosyne before it ran into Lethe's river.

Lethe screamed, rising from the waters as if burned. "You," she said. "You are early."

"I am years too late."

And Lethe smiled. A secret, scary smile, and somewhere in the darkness, Hera heard a scream.

"My mother will be so displeased," Lethe said, laughing.

"I did this for him." Hera stared at the river that had given her happiness in the emptiness of forgetting. "But no longer."

With a thought, she was in the field, striding toward Hebe, who stared at her and said, "Mother, you're crying."

"No. I'm not." Hera wiped her eyes savagely. She was not crying. She would never cry again.

Turning for home, she let the horses pick their way up Mount Olympus.

Zeus was waiting on one of the balconies. "My darling," he said, taking her in his arms.

It had only been a few weeks since she last drank Lethe's water. It had taken him so little time to get tired of her.

She let him hold her one last time. Then she whispered, "You smell of wood nymphs. Of demigoddess. Of humans. Of swans and lovely, willowy creatures who you should not touch. You reek of all of them, my husband. And you make me sick."

He let her go. "And you reek of Mnemosyne's river."

"You prefer I stink of Lethe's?" Backing away from him, she held her head high. "I can't stop what you do. I can't make you a different man. But I can choose what I know and what I don't."

"Hera -- "

"No. I choose, not you. And I choose to remember everything."

For a moment, he seemed to be considering ways to win her back. His smile was fixed in place and he held his hand out to her.

"I choose."

The smile faded, and she saw his true face. His voice was harsh and low as he said, "You will not like living this way."

"You are no doubt right."

The look he gave her was full of hatred, and she imagined it always would be.

She found she could live with that

"HERA"
by Alexis Viorsdottir

APOLOGIA

HEARTACHE OF THE CUCKOO
by Melia Suez

The cuckoo (kokux in Greek) is a small, shy migratory bird in Europe and Asia. It has an interesting habit. It lays its egg(s) in other birds' nest -- as in birds of different species. When the cuckoo chick hatches, it shoves the other eggs or foster-siblings out of the nest. The cuckoo chick is then the sole recipient of food from the adult bird(s) of the differing species. Mama cuckoo gets to produce young yet not have to work to raise them and dad never even sees the egg; this may have caused some ancients to think that the shy cuckoo self-reproduces.

Cuckoos are a bird that signals the start of spring. It is associated with spring rains, thunderstorms and plough time. It is from them that the word cuckold derives. Cuckoos have been called indiscreet observers and agents in covert affairs. They can represent the absent spouse, hidden lover, traveler or adulterous mate. Cuckoos are a phallic symbol. It is said that the number of their calls can predict the number of years left in your life, in your marriage or until you have children. Predictably, this made the cuckoo an animal associated with Hera in imagery.

"The statue of Hera is seated on a throne; it is huge, made of gold and ivory, and is a work of Polycleitus. She is wearing a crown with Graces and Seasons worked upon it, and in one hand she carries a pomegranate and in the other a sceptre. About the pomegranate I must say nothing, for its story is somewhat of a holy mystery. The presence of a cuckoo seated on the sceptre they explain by the story that when Zeus was in love with Hera in her maidenhood he changed himself into this bird, and she caught it to be her pet. This tale and similar legends about the gods I relate without believing them, but I relate them nevertheless." Pausanias 2.17.4

As far as I can find this is the only surviving text that speaks of this myth. I want you to note, at no point in the text does it say that Zeus raped or ravished her. Turning into the bird was the only way he could get close enough to woo her as Hera had been avoiding him as she refused to give into his sexual overtures until he married her. After their marriage they had a honeymoon that lasted three hundred years. Mythologically speaking, the cuckoo seems to describe Zeus more so than Hera. So why is this bird associated so strongly with Hera?

Hera may have been associated with the cuckoo out of a sense of romance and the advantages it brought her. Because of it, she became Queen of the Gods, Goddess of Marriage, Fidelity, Women and their fertility. Among her duties was overseeing childbirth and the begetting of legitimate heirs. Myths say that it is through her marriage that she gained a position of power in the Olympian hierarchy. Yet by being associated with that bird of omen she was set on track for difficulties and heartache.

Just as cuckoos heralded spring and regeneration, each year Hera would regenerate her maidenhood. As cuckoos deceive other birds, so Hera deceives Zeus (the borrowing Aphrodite's girdle to distract him being a prime example). As the female cuckoo seemed to the ancients to reproduce without a partner, so Hera reproduced at least one child without the aid of Zeus. As non-biological parents raise the cuckoo chick, so did Hera often leave, or appear to leave, the raising of her children to others. Hephaistos was given to Thetis; and according to Lucian, Ares to Priapus who taught him to dance before learning martial arts. However, admittedly I find nothing on the raising of Hebe, so this may be an exception. Hera was also known for dropping young gods and heroes, like Dionysos and Herakles, into situations to see how they would extricate themselves, not unlike leaving a young bird in a nest of strangers.

121

Yet, according to myth, Hera was also on the negative receiving end of the cuckoo omen with all the affairs that were attributed to Zeus. I think these myths are more indicative of ancient Greek culture, titillation and the appeal of divine origins. They are not about who Zeus is or who Hera is but about how Greek society saw them to be based upon their own actions.

Modern sensibilities are often offended by "adulterer" Zeus and feel pity for Hera. Yet one needs to have an understanding of the views of the ancient Greeks to even begin to understand these myths. For men, marital fidelity was unnecessary. Married men who had sex with another, male or female, citizen or citizen's female charge, slave or prostitute, did not constitute adultery. The main concern was with the woman and whether she was married or marriageable. Inheritance and citizenship laws made knowledge of the paternity of children a necessity. This meant the chastity of a woman was of the utmost importance. She was expected to maintain her and her family's reputation by being sexually modest. When a liaison was discovered, typically the adulterer was only fined or publicly humiliated. Occasionally in a fit of angry passion, they may have been injured or killed or even subjected to extortion. The female was divorced if married and unable to participate in public religious life. A single female was considered "soiled" and unmarriageable; consequently, she was thrown out of the household or sold into slavery. Conversely, an adulterer was seen as socially disruptive and a threat to family stability, yet his virility was also enhanced.

This was a very dishonorable matter for the citizen who was in charge of that female. It was a major loss of social recognition and a slur against his masculinity as it meant that he could not properly guard the females under his protection. Such seductions were considered worse than rape because they were done with the complicity of the female. This could result in the passing off of an illegitimate child as belonging to the husband, therefore "polluting" the family line. If it was the citizen's mother, then it put his own legitimacy in doubt. Yet such clandestine relationships were not unusual due to the prevalence of arranged marriages.

Zeus as King of the Gods had to be seen as virile to be a truly great divine king. So the myths have him seduce women left and right to prove this virility. Having Zeus show up in strange guises, as a shower of gold, a snake, a bull, et cetera served to even further his wily reputation. It was even better to have his progeny infiltrate family lines. This not only makes a mockery of the human male but also gives succeeding generations divine origins and a sense of entitlement over their more "common" brethren. Zeus' reputation was enhanced even more by having his wife be modest and protected, even jealous of the marital rights that he continually ignores. The only way Hera, or any mortal woman of the time, could avenge themselves was through punishing the women or the children of these relationships. Mythological Hera was well known for the fury she unleashed in both cases. For example, in the myths, Phthonos seems to have been a constant, yet rarely mentioned, companion of Hera. Phthonos (or Zelos) is the Greek daimon of jealousy and envy particularly where love is concerned. To the Romans, the daimon was Invidia. Both divinities were associated with the "evil eye." One who looks upon another with jealousy or envy was said to have cast the evil eye, causing many problems for the recipient. Plutarch described these looks as poisoned darts sent out in one's gaze. Democritus described them as envious particles full of poison, which damage the bodies and minds of whoever had to the misfortune of being on the receiving end. In this context she is mainly portrayed as the punisher of her husband's paramours or the children resulting from these unions. This is another indication that these myths are more indicative of the ancient Greek culture than of the goddess.

In ancient times, it was extremely difficult for a woman to divorce her husband, yet it was quite easy for a man to divorce his wife. All he had to do was reject her in front of witnesses or return her to her father's home along with her dowry, which did not include their children. On the other hand, a woman had to convince an official that the divorce was needed, but the likelihood of another male interfering in another man's household was slim. Her husband could prevent her from meeting with an official simply by forbidding her to leave the house. Because a man could easily dismiss his wife, jealousy and fear were ensured on her part whenever he was in the mere presence of another woman. What if he likes her more? What if their union produced a child and that was a boy? What if her children were healthier or more robust or simply more favored? Another woman put the wife's status, life, and children in danger.

Depending on the myth, either Zeus and Hera produced no male children together or they were despised (in the case of Ares) or rejected (Hephaistos due to his imperfect physical form). Since Zeus could divorce her at any time, Hera was understandably fearful of losing her marriage, her home and the power it brought her. So many tales revolve around Hera hassling Zeus' lovers or harrying the sons of these unions. Off the top of my head I can't think of a single instance of her hassling daughters. In reality, Hera has nothing to fear. She is a powerful immortal in her own right. Even if the unthinkable were to happen, Hera would have been fine on her own unlike the women of ancient Greece. Such jealousies humanized the goddess of marriage and women in the eyes of her female worshipers.

Yet what about fidelity? Fidelity is implicit in any good relationship whether it is between husband and wife, friends, business partners or even countries. Trust, faith, abiding by your promises, et cetera; these are all important aspects of good working relationships. Zeus has many epithets that relate to fidelity, on both personal and political fronts: Asbamaios (Keeper of Oaths), Euxeinos (the Hospitable), Gamelios (of Marriage), Hetaireios (of Fellowship), Horkios (Protector of Oaths), Kolastes (Punisher of Hubris), Pater (Father), Philios (of

Friendship), Pistios (of Faith and Fidelity), Xenios (Protector of Hospitality), Zugious (of Marriage), Zyius (Uniter), and so on. Hera's epithets reflect the same: Gamelii (of Marriage), Teleia (Fulfiller), Zygia (of Marriage), et cetera. Therefore, these adulterous myths are more about the ancient Greek society and less about Zeus and Hera in reality. To truly begin to understand either one of them, one needs to remove the blinding image imposed by ancient Greek myths. One needs to remove the biases that our own Christianized culture has placed upon Zeus especially. Likewise, these myths have done nothing to aid Hera's reputation, as they portray her as little more than a jealous shrew.

When the seed of a relationship is planted, friendship/lust/love/need is the catalyst that starts the roots of the relationship, no matter the type of relationship. That is what Aphrodite is … she is the catalyst. But for the relationship to survive it needs commitment and that is what Hera is. For the relationship to grow beyond the sunny days of laughter and good times, through the rain of tears and the dark nights of uncertainty, jealousy and anger, it takes commitment. Aphrodite still keeps the relationship fertile but for the growth to happen and continue it requires Hera's patience and commitment. A relationship can have all the love in the world, but without the commitment to see it through it will die when the excitement and newness wear off. That can take weeks, months or even years, but if the commitment isn't there, eventually the relationship will not be either.

QUEEN OF KINÊSIS:
UNDERSTANDING HERA
by Edward P. Butler

In the Platonic interpretation of the Hellenic pantheon, Hera appears as coequal with Zeus in the organization of the cosmos on the highest intellective plane, which is the most universal intellective organization of things. The core of this intellective organization is the operational tetrad formed by Kronos, Rhea, Zeus and Hera, while the other children of Kronos and Rhea, together with the children of Zeus, organize the cosmos from the hypercosmic plane just below. One of the ways Platonists justify this placement is by citing Iliad I 547-8, where Zeus says to Hera that "Whatever it is fitting that you should hear [of what I plan to do], this no other, whether of Gods or of humans, will know before you" (trans. Murray). The Platonist Proclus emphasizes the equality of Zeus and Hera, stating in his commentary on Plato's *Timaios* that "Hera proceeds together with Zeus, bringing to birth all things together with [him]" (In Tim. I, 46), and again that the chief demiurge, or artisan, of the world-order, "who is the great Zeus, is conjoined with Hera; hence she is said to be equal in rank [*isotelês*] with him" (IT I, 450). The hypercosmic Gods, who are active on the succeeding plane, concern themselves with the approximation of beings to forms, while Zeus and Hera are responsible for the original formalization or articulation of the continuum of Being. The ground is laid for this formalization in many ways by the prior orders of Gods; but it is the work of Zeus and Hera especially which will produce the conditions for thought as such. Thought requires a thinker, that is, a soul, and an idea; and we may say that Zeus is particularly responsible for the latter, Hera for the former.

The principal technical determinations according to which Platonists understand Hera's role are motion (*kinêsis*) and the mixing vessel (*kratêr*, from *krasis*, mixing or blending).

When, in Plato's dialogue the Parmenides, it is denied that the One is in motion (Parm. 138b & sqq.), it means that no God or Goddess, qua deity, is in motion, but also that a certain class of Gods are the causes of motion to all things that do move. Motion is of two types, alteration and spatial motion, while the latter in turn is divided into circular motion, which can be eternal, and rectilinear motion, which is necessarily finite. The Platonist's concept of motion is not that of the modern physicist, for it is wider, encompassing ideal motion prior to soul.(1) For the Platonist, for example, there is a kind of 'motion' inherent in reason, even without a reasoner; there is motion in a sequence, even prior to the time in which it would unfold; there is motion in the reciprocal relations between units in a manifold, without need that these objects be physical. The primordial forms of motion are constituted on the intelligible-intellective plane, prior to the intellective plane where Zeus and Hera are active. The intelligible-intellective plane is the hypostasis of Life (*Zôê*), and is formed by the activities of Gods such as Ouranos and Gaia, its wisdom delivered through the oracle of Nyx, its ongoing presence on subsequent planes secured by Aphrodite, the only child of Ouranos who is counted not among the Titans but among the Olympians. All that lives, moves, and all that moves, lives in some sense, even if in a dependent fashion or in a way we may consider metaphorical; hence the deities of the intellective class who particularly carry forward the project of the hypostasis of Life are classed as life-giving or vivific (*zoogonic*). The highest of these vivific divinities in the Hellenic pantheon are Rhea and her daughter Hera.

To understand more closely Hera's specific role, we must turn to another dialogue, the *Timaios*. Platonists identify Hera with the mixing vessel or *kratêr* in which the elements of the soul of the cosmos and every individual soul as well are combined by the action of the demiurge, whom Platonists identify with Hellenic Zeus. Plato himself does not personify the mixing vessel, any more than he explicitly identifies the demiurge with Zeus. These identifications came later, in accord with the ongoing Platonic project of arriving at a conceptual grasp of Hellenic theology. The identification of Hera with the *kratêr*, therefore, comes out of a prior determination regarding Hera's importance in the generation of the soul. A distinctive characteristic of the *Timaios* cosmogony is its resistance to the concept of creation as such. Instead, all the processes it describes give order to elements and forces that already exist and are somehow already in play. The demiurge receives a universe that is already visible, and is already in motion, albeit in a disorderly and discordant fashion (Tim. 30a). The demiurge thus does not create the universe, but rather offers to it an ideal. Given that the *Timaios* cosmogony begins from the middle of things in this fashion, mediating agencies such as the mixing vessel seem to express the very nature of the cosmogony itself. The *chôra* or 'space' that serves as 'the wetnurse of becoming' (Tim. 52d) is another example of such an agency in the *Timaios* account, one which has received far more attention in modern literature on the *Timaios* than has the *kratêr*. The lack of an explicitly conceptual account of the mixing vessel in the *Timaios*, however, suggests that explication of its nature is to be found elsewhere, and indeed, we shall see that the myths provide this indispensable supplement.

The generation of the soul in the *Timaios* occurs in two stages: first the demiurge blends the elements of the universal soul (Tim. 35a-37c), then, in "the former bowl, wherein he had blended and mixed the soul of the universe" (41d), the demiurge produces individual souls from the same materials. The soul's constituents are Identity, Difference, and divisible and indivisible Being. The soul is thus made of no simple materials, but of purely relative or relational determinations, and in this way the mixing vessel virtually is the psychogony itself, because such relations are inconceivable without a medium of encounter, and even of conflict -- Identity and Difference, in particular, are "difficult to mix" (Tim. 35a). But the mixing vessel involves as well the cooperative dimensions of divine relations, for the Platonist Proclus remarks (attributing the insight to his teacher Syrianus) that what theologies express through marriages and offspring among the Gods is expressed by Plato through the concept of mixture (In Tim. III, 248). Indeed, it is appropriate that marriage should be treated as the primary theological symbol of ontological mixture insofar as that mixture is identified with Hera, patron Goddess of marriage. Proclus provides further specifications and delimitations of the activity of the mixing vessel, explaining that the *kratêr* is "the cause of souls so far as they are souls, and not of all life, for it is neither the cause of intellective, nor of physical life" (IT III, 250) -- i.e., angelical and daimonical life, on the one hand, and purely biological life on the other, which are attributed by him to Rhea (ibid., 248). Furthermore, the constitution of the soul of the universe is attributed more to the demiurge, the constitution of the individual souls more to the *kratêr*. With respect to the next generation of Olympians, a distinction is drawn by Proclus between Hera's rational vivification and the physical vivification Artemis provides (IT I, 79), in conjunction with Rhea as the more universal vivific divinity. Some of these specifications will take on a more than technical significance when surveyed in the light of the myths.

A final important Platonic designation of Hera comes from the Phaedrus, in which the effect of Hera upon her worshipers is described. For those unfamiliar with this dialogue, Socrates explains how those who have been 'followers' of diverse deities prior to birth, when their souls traveled in the supracelestial place, manifest that allegiance in life through their patterns of erotic attachment, in what sort of human they find attractive and in their style of love. In this context, Socrates states that "Those who were in the train of Hera look for a royal [basilikon] nature, and when they have found such a one, they act in a corresponding manner toward him in all respects" (253b). This resonates strongly with something said of Zeus in Plato's Philebus, which states that "Through the power of causality [dia tên tês aitias dunamin] there is in the nature [phusis] of Zeus a royal soul and a royal intellect" (30d). This demonstrates how closely knit was Plato's own thought about the Olympians, and how far from a collection of casual allusions and metaphors. Such remarks take on a special significance because in such passages Plato himself speaks directly of Hera and of Zeus, unlike the conceptual determinations of divine activity imparted in dialogues such as the *Parmenides* or the *Timaios*, which later Platonists attribute to the Olympians through a deductive procedure. Like Hera's mortal 'followers', Zeus's exercise of his own causal power or agency is affected by his *eros* for Hera, his sister, spouse and co-sovereign. Her causality lends to his intellect and soul her characteristic 'royal' aspect, and ensures that the evolution of the cosmos will include the development of forms of sovereignty and political life expressing her nature, as we shall see.

On the most general level, Platonists interpret the elaborate mythic narratives concerning the activities of the Olympians after Zeus has established his sovereignty as dealing with the constitution of the universal soul and with the constitution of the many different kinds and conditions of particular souls. The interrelations of the Olympians, specifically, generate the characteristics of the universal soul, while their relations with heroes and other mortals in the myths are generative of types of soul as well as worldly institutions shaping particular souls. Insofar as these are also the two operations performed by the demiurge with the *kratêr* in the *Timaios*, the marriage of Zeus and Hera that is thus symbolized can be seen also to encompass and symbolize the whole of this subsequent body of mythic narrative, and all of the Hellenic myths taking place after this event can hence be treated as a single narrative, the story of Zeus and Hera's partnership. It is a challenge to adopt this perspective on the myths; hence I wish in the remainder of this essay to offer tools to facilitate understanding Hera's activity in all of the myths in which she occurs, as well as devoting particular attention to some in which she plays a special role.

A primary issue arising with respect to the myths we possess featuring Hera is the appearance in them of manifestations of her 'wrath'. Anthropomorphic explanations of this attribute are, I believe, especially detrimental insofar as these explanations evoke further, sympathetic passions in response. One may simply reject the representation of the Gods as suffering such passions. But the option also exists of a symbolic interpretation of these mythic passions. Proclus explains that Hera is "the source of all the Titanic division [*diairesis*] perceived in souls according to destiny [*moiras*], and the cause of distinction [*diakrisis*]" (In Tim. III, 249). In effect, Zeus has more to do with what souls have in common, and Hera more with that in which they differ, with the things that draw souls apart, and often into conflict. This was already suggested by the distinction drawn between the generation of the soul of the cosmos, attributed more to the demiurge, and the generation of particular souls, attributed more to the mixing vessel, the arena of encounter. The conflict on this plane is necessary, insofar as some things have to be in conflict sometimes in order to fully manifest themselves according to their peculiar destiny and find their niche in a complex world, and the conflict the myths express between Zeus and Hera is part of driving forward this process of manifestation.

We can see this clearly in one of the most common sources for mythic conflict between Zeus and Hera, namely Zeus's 'infidelities'. In Platonic thought the primary form of causality is symbolically erotic, for it expresses the perception of the Good in its primary articulation, namely Beauty of every kind. As the universal demiurge, Zeus is erotically active throughout his realm. His mythic dalliances are in this way equivalent to the abstract determination of the demiurge's activity in the *Timaios*, in which we read that the demiurge organizes the cosmos according to his vision of "the most beautiful intelligible" (Tim. 30d), that is to say, according to his experience of beauty as such, for he is "the best of causes" (29a). The planes of being which emerge from this activity of Zeus, however, cannot be collapsed into one another merely on the basis of this common causal element, lest the opportunities for diverse manifestation be diminished. Note, in this respect, the two instances in which Zeus does 'absorb' another. In the Orphic cosmogony, he completely assimilates Phanes, the primary intelligible, identified by Platonists with the universal paradigm of the *Timaios*, because on the most universal level, intellect incorporates its object without remainder, although from other perspectives there are many points on which the object escapes its grasp. In the second instance, Zeus absorbs Metis, subsequently giving birth himself to Athena, because the matters with which Athena concerns herself, though they lie on lower planes of being, demand an intellectual integrity that must to some degree override the differences of particular cases: this is the formal problem of justice. Hera, by contrast, in 'disapproving' of these actions of Zeus, symbolically and actually maintains the distinctions between the different planes of being mediated by his *eros*, and her 'wrath' causes a series of events that further articulate the planes in question. Moreover, because Hera's conflicts are chiefly with Zeus, the conflicts concern more universal, and thus more basic, properties and activities of souls than the conflicts arising among the other Olympians, which it falls often to Zeus to mediate through some suitable apportionment of honors [*timai*], whereas there is generally no mediator between Zeus and Hera in their own conflicts.

Hence the strife between Zeus and Hera is truly, as Hephaestus says in the Iliad, "for mortals' sakes" (Il. 1.574). Indeed, bringing forth the mortal world is in itself in a certain respect a "work of sorrow" (573). To better understand Hera's myths, in fact, we must attempt to better understand the entire phenomenon of Gods experiencing passions in mythic narratives, for example, Hera's pity in the first book of the Iliad, which parallels Apollo's wrath (55-56). One of the principal theological messages of the *Iliad* is that the Gods experience passions in the constitution of our own, impassioned plane of Being, and that this experience is inseparable in certain ways from divine action on this plane. Perhaps the most extreme example of this is when Aphrodite is wounded rescuing Aineias in the Iliad (5.335 & sq.). In book one, Hera pities the Danaans, it is explained, because she sees [*horato*] them dying. Seeing is the most basic passion or passivity: Hera exposes herself to the vision of the mortals, though this is a mode of knowledge that as a Goddess she transcends, possessing far more effective means of insight into the nature of the world. From this passion, however, she formulates an intention of a form suitable to arise directly in the mind (epi phresi (55)) of one who ordinarily experiences things in this fashion: Hera's pity causes her to put in Achilles's mind the impulse to act, to call an assembly. The passions of the Gods are thus in themselves actions: the wrath of Apollo is the dying of mortals by pestilence, the seeing of mortal suffering is Hera's action upon the mind of Achilles.

A particular passion with which Hera is causally associated in myths such as those of Herakles or of Io is insanity, an appropriately intellective passion to be produced by the Queen of Intellect. Proclus says that the myths designate Hera "the cause of insanity [mania], but Zeus of temperance [*sôphrosunê*]; and the former, of labors in the realm of becoming, but the latter, of leading up from it [*anagôgê*]. For Hera excites all things to procession, multiplies them, and causes them by her illuminations to be prolific" (In Tim. III, 251). The insanity of Herakles or of Io, which are attributed to Hera, are thus symbols of the procession of soul into the physical realm, away from the realm of pure Mind and thus, by definition, in the direction of 'insanity'. By causing 'insanity' in Herakles, Hera leads him to the performance of labors that result in new possibilities for humanity; they are labors of civilization. The myths symbolize the cause of this as insanity because 'sanity' for souls lies in turning oneself back toward the sources of one's being. In this sense, it is 'insane' to be concerned with going deeper into the world of conflict. It is not, therefore, that the insanity Hera causes in Herakles has the ancillary benefit of causing his civilizing labors: rather, Herakles's labors and his insanity are symbolically one and the same. Heroic action is in a certain sense, then, linked to divine passion. What the Gods

133

accomplish at their most passive, a special mortal, a hero, does at their most active. Indeed, this is how we may understand the symbol of the divine parentage of the hero. Zeus, through his passions with respect to mortals, fathers many heroes and has an embodied presence on the mortal plane through them, while Hera's involvement on this plane of manifestation is expressed rather through her own passions and the passions she incites in mortal beings.

There is a certain convergence between Hera and Dionysos inasmuch as both are known to provoke episodic insanity. It is not unusual for Heraic madness to be directly identified with Bacchic frenzy.(2) Plato (Laws 627b) and Apollodorus (Bibliotheca 3.33) both trace the origin of Bacchic frenzy to an episode of insanity imposed upon Dionysos by Hera; Aeschylus calls Io a "maenad of Hera"; Euripides characterizes Herakles's insanity as Bacchic frenzy. Heraic and Dionysiac madness seem thus to be regarded as essentially the same phenomenon from a descriptive point of view. Nor do either Hera or Dionysos have to be involved; the madness of Orestes, caused by the Furies, is also described as Bacchic frenzy. Theologically, then, it makes no sense to characterize Dionysos and Hera as "natural enemies", as Seaford does (135). On the contrary, it seems that there is an important overlap in their functions relative to the emergence of the soul. Insanity can be seen as symbolically expressing the formal differentiation of the soul into its diverse, and potentially conflicting, faculties. Insofar as Hera has a broader sphere of activity than Dionysos, however, her functions with respect to the soul's formal differentiation extend beyond the confines of the Bacchic frenzy she causes in common with Dionysos. Perusing diverse instances of Hera's 'wrath', one can see that even where her wrathful actions don't involve causing insanity, they can be read as concerning soul's formal differentiation.

Let us take as an example the Sphinx Hera visits upon Thebes. The Sphinx herself, like most mythical composite beasts, enacts the differentiated soul, with her blend of human, lion, and eagle parts -- compare Plato's image of the human soul as containing a human (the intelligence), a lion (the 'spirited' part), and a many-headed beast (the desiring part) (Rep. 588b & sq.). The parentage of the Sphinx traces back, either in the first or the second generation, to Typhoeus/Typhaon/Typhon, who is either the offspring of Hera herself, in a parthenogenesis mirroring the birth of Athena from Zeus, or of Gaia alone, or of Gaia and Tartaros. Typhon is associated with the dense atmospheric phenomena of smoke or storms, the counterpart to Zeus's association with lightning; note that Hera's eidolon, or phantom double, is Nephele (Latin Nebula), 'cloud'. Hera and Typhon are therefore both associated with phenomena in which the airy medium becomes dense enough to be visible in itself. What lightning is to Zeus, mist is to Hera. Insofar as Hera's sphere of action is soul, these are circumstances in which the psychical medium becomes itself the agent, as when emotion supersedes intention. (When Typhon's parentage is traced to Gaia instead, the soul's 'weather', with all the same traits, is grounded in wider cosmic factors.) Zeus's lightning, by contrast, of which Herakleitos says "Lightning steers all things" (D. 64), creates a momentary flash of illumination in which everything appears, if only for an instant; the next generation of Olympians will secure the means to sustain illumination. Typhon, by collecting in his person the stormy forces of the soul, thus actually contributes to Athena's emancipation of intention from its concrete circumstances, freeing the space of justice and law, and we may understand their explicit complementarity in this fashion.

The Sphinx, therefore, being in the line of Typhon, is a further concrete expression of the causality inherent in the psychic medium as such. The soul is depicted thus as a set of diverse faculties held in suspension, and a nature at once wise, riddling, and violent. The narrative context of the Sphinx is that of an 'injustice' of some sort that attaches to the city of Thebes as a whole. One should read any 'injustice' in myth through the lens of Anaximander's fragment, which states that "the source of coming-to-be for existing things is that into which

135

destruction, too, happens, according to necessity; for they pay penalty and retribution to each other for their injustice according to the assessment of Time".(3) 'Injustice' in myths is almost always a question of the emergence of some structure whose incorporated energy will have to be 'paid back'. One might compare the modern concept of negative entropy, according to which living systems need to 'export' their disorder.

This structure is the key, I think, to unlocking much of the symbolic richness in narrative itself. Since divine 'wrath' in a myth so often goes together with a narrative about 'injustice', it should come as no surprise that divine 'wrath' is essentially productive of such negentropic structures, and that so much of the innovation that occurs on the material plane in myths does so as a result of divine 'wrath', and why 'wrathful' deities in cultures such as Egypt and India are so often the deities not of last but of first resort. Divine 'wrath' of this sort is productive specifically of things that possess this negentropic tension and thus 'pay penalty … according to the assessment of Time'; and the Sphinx's riddle to Oedipus concerns the mortal soul's temporal differentiation: first an infant, now an adult in the prime of life, then elderly.

The whole work performed by the demiurge in giving order to the cosmos can virtually be reduced to the single concept of temporalization, i.e., creating a "moving image of eternity" (Tim. 37d). This is not a question of putting something static into motion, but of giving a measure to eternally existing motion; hence the demiurge's act is inseparable from the emergence of soul as the locus of measurement, making sense of the continuum of experience to which it is subject. This is the kernel of truth in the doctrine of Protagoras and other sophists that humans are the measure of all things, "of the things that are, that/how they are, and of things that are not, that/how they are not". Through the patterning of time, demiurgy enacts its world-order. These world-orders in turn are not passive embodiments of a culture, or a linguistic or geographical territory, but rather the enactment of these territories; they are what is living in these territories. These world-views or world-orders are the souls of which the cultural territories we can observe are the bodies. In this sense, the Sphinx enacts a certain phase of the Theban polis as a living cultural and juridical entity, and is a particularly clear example of the role of Hera as a vivific intellective deity. The entity thus ensouled is a whole of which some mortal bodies form parts, an animal made up of animals, and sharing to some extent a common destiny, as we see in the collective drama of the Theban polis as it plays out right through the generation of the children of Oedipus. That Thebes should come to be politically ensouled, as such, as a 'punishment' is no different than the way in which the institution of totemic organizations is mythically attributed to a sequence of 'injustice' and 'retribution', embodying the negentropic temporality instituted by the traditions, initiations, taboos and so forth, whose origin is described in such a narrative. Once again, therefore, divine passions in myth are also heroic, culture-founding actions. Moreover, Hera's association with sovereignty, her 'queenly' dimension, in this way connects with her association with the demiurgic 'vessel' in the *Timaios*, through the notion of 'vessels' intermediate in scope between the individual soul and the cosmic animal, namely the 'body politic' constituted over a particular region of space and time.

I would like to conclude this sketch, for it cannot claim to be more than that, of Hera's role in Hellenic theology, with a discussion of a mythic cycle in which Hera is evidently important, namely the cycle that begins with Ixion and ends with Jason and the Argonauts. This cycle actually begins properly from Ixion's father Phlegyas, whose name means 'fiery'. Both of Phlegyas's children have important dealings with the Olympians. His daughter Koronis ('crow') conceives Asklepios by Apollon and gives birth to him from her flaming corpse, establishing a parallel between Asklepios and Dionysos that seems to be in Pindar's mind, as well, when he evokes Kadmos and his daughters toward the end of the same ode where he recounts the birth of Dionysos (Pythian Ode III). A fiery fate awaits Ixion, too, after he has burned alive his wife's father. Absolved by Zeus, Ixion attends an Olympian banquet and, seized by desire for Hera, formulates the intention to seduce her. But Zeus thwarts him, and instead, it is a cloud-double of Hera, Nephele, with whom Ixion mates and fathers Kentauros, the eponymous ancestor of the Centaurs. Ixion is famously fastened to a revolving fiery wheel in the sky as punishment, while Nephele subsequently becomes the mother of the twins Phrixos and Helle, who ride a flying golden ram to Kolchis. It is the fleece of this ram, finally, that Jason acquires on the voyage of the Argo.

Ixion's wheel may be understood as the rotation of the elements, which is for Herakleitos a series of states of fire, for the cosmos is "everliving fire, kindling in measures and going out in measures" (D. 30).(4) In this process, the other elements are produced: "Fire's turnings [*tropai*]: first sea, and of sea the half is earth, the half storm [*prêstêr*, i.e., wind and lightning] ... <earth> is dispersed as sea, and is measured so as to form the same proportion as existed before it became earth" (D. 31). Fire retains a kind of self-identity in its transformations, however, in that "All things are an equal exchange for fire and fire for all things, as goods are for gold and gold for goods" (D. 90). For Herakleitos this cosmic order has no single author, no God or human made it (D. 30); rather, it has come about purely through strife (D. 80), rather than any plan, and this is the nature of fire, which is not so much a concrete element as a process of consuming and transforming its fuel.

The 'turnings' of fire that begin with Phlegyas, and that include the burning of Koronis at the birth of Asklepios, are themselves embodied in Ixion's wheel. Ixion's burning lust for Hera embodies the investment, so to speak, of metaphysical fire through passion and its consequent cycle of transformations in embodiment: it is psychogony itself. Empedokles says of the

138

soul, once it has "put its trust in raving Strife", that "the force of the *aithêr* pursues him into the sea, the sea spews him out onto the floor of the earth, the earth casts him into the rays of the blazing sun, and the sun into the eddies of the air" (D. 115), an elemental 'wheel' akin to Ixion's in origin and effect.

The element of air is glimpsed first in this cycle in the identification of Koronis with the crow, sometimes underscored by the presence in the myth of an actual crow who is turned from white to black in the process. Air becomes thematic in the myth, however, with the introduction of Nephele. The cloud of which Nephele is formed concretizes the airy medium, akin to Typhon, as noted above. It was common in antiquity to associate Hera's very name with *aêr*, a word which connotes, not so much the pure atmosphere with which we tend to associate our word 'air', but with the weather's many moods. As the substrate of weather, air's plasticity gives it a living quality even before we conceive it as the lifegiving root of soul as breath and of intelligence as 'inspiration'. The philosopher Anaximenes could treat air as the principle or *archê* of the cosmos primarily because of this power of condensation and rarefaction, which is symbolized in its purest form in the creation of Nephele. Zeus creates Nephele at once as image of Hera, a vessel for her divinity, and as an airy trap that binds Ixion's fiery desire into a cyclical motion, an operation anticipating the ensouling work of the Platonic demiurge. With Nephele's marriage to Athamas, though, the myth turns to the social and political plane.

In the triangle of Athamas, Nephele, and Ino, Phrixos and Helle are placed in the crucible, at risk of sacrifice because of a collective failure embodied by the parching of the seed-grain, a subversion of the community's future symbolically equivalent to the attempted sacrifice of the young heir to the throne. As in the case of the Theban Sphinx, it appears that a polity, a negentropic 'body politic', comes to birth here through a crisis. A symbolic equation can be drawn between the advent of the golden flying ram, a sky-shining symbol of sovereignty,

139

to rescue Nephele's children, and Ino, their tormentor, but also an original bacchant, whose destiny is fulfilled at last as a shining Goddess of the sea, Leukothea ('White Goddess'). On the political plane, the bacchic function embodies the sovereignty of the masses, the crowd, which intertwines very closely with Hera's political functions. The presence of Dionysos on the periphery of this myth fills the void of sovereignty created by the discrediting of Athamas, a void that will not be fully remedied, however, until the golden fleece returns. Dionysos, as the always-future sovereign of the cosmos, hence never present intact, frequently manifests where the polity suffers an interregnum of legitimate authority. A fleece was one of the items with which the Titans beguiled the Dionysos child before murdering him and, as a skin, is a general symbol of embodiment or investment, an embodiment that is collective and political in this myth, in accord with Hera's tendency to direct eros toward sovereignty.

The episode with Phrixos and Helle bears some time later, when Hera's wrath comes to be directed at Pelias, a son of Poseidon, while the instrument of her vengeance is Jason, the fully mortal grandson of Pelias's mother Tyro. Jason's story is thus notable in the first place for its inversion of the mythic structure which has at its center the child of a mortal and a deity, for here the 'hero', ontologically speaking, is not the 'hero' of the narrative, but its villain. Hera is the patron of the Argo and its voyage, though her overt interventions in the *Argonautika* are few. Once we have a sense for Hera's role as psychogonic demiurge, however, we can appreciate how the entire myth is hers. The *Argonautika* is a journey of the soul to the sources of its being. The Argo's very wood -- in Greek the term hylê means at first 'wood' but comes to mean 'matter' -- possesses the power of speech, and so the vessel constitutes a single mind, its heroic crew its diverse powers. The Argo voyages east to a land ruled by a son of Helios, and so to the rising sun itself, suggesting a reversal of the flow of time. Temporal regression and explanatory regression are symbolically interchangeable in Hellenic thought. Jason is,

140

according to his name, a healing agent, a cure. As such, the voyage of the Argo is not about the ultimate or categorical origins of the mortal soul -- this, we have seen, was treated in the portion of the cycle concerning Ixion and Nephele -- so much as a therapeutic action on behalf of the soul already constituted. We have already seen the theme of healing arise in the collateral descent from Phlegyas through Ixion's sister Koronis and thus to Asklepios, who, like Jason, is reared by Cheiron the centaur. Furthermore, Jason brings home with him, in addition to the fleece, Medea, whose name is associated with mêdomai, to plan,(5) and whose mother's name is Iduia, 'Knower'. The Argo thus achieves understanding of the soul's origin/principle for the sake of healing.

Another dimension of the Argo's voyage concerns Hera's primary Platonic attribution of motion. Hellenic philosophers distinguish between the motions of locomotion and alteration, and within locomotion, between circular and rectilinear motion. Circular motion has the character of intelligibility, because repetition, or at least repeatability, is essential to conceptualization. Hence the mortal being as a particular of some species has a finite, and thus rectilinear path, but the species ideally repeats itself, and the many such natural cycles, together with the cycles of the heavens, give to time a circular characteristic. The Argo's voyage, however, is both circular and linear: circular, in that it returns to the point it started from, but linear in the sense that the routes to and from Kolchis share no points in common, despite the geographical extravagances in which the story thus involves its narrators. The Argo must encounter only the new until it arrives back at Iolkos, and in this way its voyage combines the circular and the linear. This characteristic provides a means for structurally differentiating the *Argonautika* from the *Odyssey*, if indeed, as Michel Serres has argued, the diverse spaces of Odysseus's journey "cannot be composed to form a single homogeneous space," and therefore the Odyssey "is not at all the story of a journey, but the journey of a story".(6) For if the topology of the *Odyssey* is peculiar to narrative as such, then the *Argonautika's* topology pertains to a different plane, determined by a different problem.

The most notable incidents on the Argo's voyage, which are consistent from one version to another, occur on the outward journey to Kolchis. Four incidents stand out in particular: the Lemnian women, the Kyzikos incident, the loss of Hylas, and the encounter with Phineus. Although other interpretations are possible, these four incidents can all be interpreted in light of basic problems of the soul in time. The Lemnian women reject their husbands and take strangers into their beds, and so what is familiar is estranged and the strange becomes familiar, while Kyzikos, who hosts the Argonauts, is unrecognized by them later and slain.

Both of these episodes appear to concern the temporal flow, which renders all things strangers to one another: "Upon those that step into the same rivers different and different waters flow ... They scatter and ... gather ... come together and flow away ... approach and depart" (*Herakleitos*, frag. D 12).(7) In the case of the Lemnian women, the results are fruitful, as befits the inaugural encounter in the tale. In the case of Kyzikos, however, the Argo lands on the same shore a second time in the night, without recognizing that it is the same. This second encounter of the story seems to underscore the importance of novelty in the Argo's journey. In order to find its way home, that is, to accomplish its goal, the Argo must stay on the path of the new; to see the same shore twice slays the particular as such. The narrative is thus set on the plane of the singular mortal individual, but structures that plane more definitely than the *Odyssey* does, because however exotic the spaces into which the Argo travels, the vessel is never not on a circular path home, just as the Argo is never without the divine voice built into its very fabric, whereas the *Odyssey*, in which the vessel as such is never really thematic, seems rather to plot a chaotic 'return' by the powers of human reason alone.(8)

142

The next established episode of the *Argonautika* concerns the loss of Hylas, which leads to Herakles's early departure; hence, it must provide some symbolic closure. To what was said above about the structure of the *Argonautika* must be added that the myth has a fractal quality, in which each episode conveys the message of the whole in its particular fashion. Herakles is in a certain respect the paradigmatic hero of the Hellenic pantheon; therefore, his experience on the Argo can be taken to represent the voyage as a whole in a certain light. Herakles's departure at this point is also traditionally linked to the planting of the first seeds of the Trojan War, interpreted by Platonists as the struggle for possession of beauty between the soul and nature, and in this way the Hylas episode gestures forward to the next generation of heroic formation of the cosmos, to which of course the *Odyssey* will also belong. The name 'Hylas' evokes *hylê*, which is 'wood' (cognate with Latin sylva), but also means 'matter' itself. Hylas is what the hero loses to embodiment. The name also suggests *hylaô*, to howl or bark, and the ritual practice of calling for Hylas is an inseparable part of the episode. The soul descends into embodiment, where the eye cannot guide one in trustworthy fashion, for the forms are obscured by mists -- hence the call, which is not articulate, however, but animalistic. Indeed, the forms on this plane are, from another viewpoint, mists themselves. As Herakleitos says, "If all things turned to smoke, the nostrils would sort them out" (D. 7), and in this the canine excels. If Zeus's forms are optical, even if only according to the eye of the soul -- hence revealed by lightning, rather than the sustained light of day -- then Hera's domain of form is these aery 'figures' especially apparent to the soul's 'canine' aspect.

The concern with sensation carries over into the episode with Phineus, which seems to complement the Hylas episode similarly to the way that the episodes of the Lemnian women and of Kyzikos complement each other. As the Lemnian women and Kyzikos concerned time in general, the episodes of Hylas and of Phineus concern sensation, which is specifically constitutive of temporal experience. Where the Hylas incident concerns sound and the notion of a 'calling', the Phineus episode is concerned with sight and with the giving of directions. Phineus is blind, the reasons for which vary in different sources. Either he has been rendered blind as a consequence of his power of prophecy, or for having shown Phrixos the way, these two evidently interchangeable; or in exchange for long life, which pertains as well to the problem of time, experience and learning; or for having blinded his sons, the grandchildren of Boreas, the North Wind, at the behest of his second wife Idaia, 'of the woods' (*idê*; compare Hylas). Phineus is plagued, in any case, by the Harpies (Harpuiai), spirits of wind gusts: again, we note Hera's association with phenomena in which the airy medium becomes concrete. In the Phineus episode, sight and wind are opposed to each other, but both fall within Hera's purview, for Hera assigns the all-seeing Argos to watch over the cow into which Io has been transformed, while Phineus is rescued by the heroes borne by the Argo -- *argos* means 'shining' or 'bright'. Why, then, is Phineus at once blind and afflicted by the Harpuiai? In interpreting myth, we ought not to choose a favored variant, but instead incorporate all variants into our interpretation.(9) Here, the variant Hesiod provides in his Catalogue of Women,(10) that Phineus traded his sight for a long life, proves valuable. If there is anything to which experience itself blinds one, it is novelty, and novelty is peculiarly demanded of the Argonauts. Hence we can understand the role of the Harpuiai, who embody impulse, their name coming from *harpazô*, to seize or snatch away. Imprisoned by his accumulation of past experience, denied the nourishing use of impulse, Phineus must be freed by the winged sons of Boreas. Hera seems absent from an episode like this until we grasp the importance of the 'airy' psychical medium in her theology, at which point we recognize her implicit presence.

Much of what is today understood as 'psychology' falls within Hera's sphere of activity, insofar as she is peculiarly concerned with the concretion of negentropic 'vessels' on scales ranging from the personal to the social-political. An important episode during the Argo's stay at Kolchis involves the sown men, who are explicitly descended from Hera via Ares, her son by Zeus. These sown men feature both in the *Argonautika* and in the myth of the Kadmean founding of Thebes. Plato also refers to such beings more than once: the creatures of the age of Kronos in the Statesman are such (Statesman 271ab), and the guardians of the city Socrates imagines in the Republic are to think of themselves in this fashion (Rep. 414de, characterized by Socrates as "a sort of Phoenician [i.e., Kadmean] tale" (414c)). The sown men are a schematic expression of the soul without history or internal complexity; it is a simple matter for Jason to make them fight one another, for this is the nature of the plane into which they are born: "War [*polemos*] is the father of all and king of all, and some he shows as Gods, others as humans; some he makes slaves, others free" (Herakleitos, fr. 53 D.). The sown men express the soul's radical origination. They are beings of pure motion or process, lacking the complex articulation of psychical functions that is peculiar to Dionysos as dismembered God. On the Argo's homeward voyage Medea dismembers her brother Apsyrtus, whose name means 'unshorn', i.e., preadolescent, like the Dionysos child who meets a similar fate. Medea thus represents the insertion of a virtual bacchic cycle within the *Argonautika*, in which the Argo's return enacts the reconstitution of the complex psyche from the seeds of living motion.

Upon her return to Hellas, Medea carries out a three part operation, according to the version recounted by Lactantius (Fabula 7, 2-4), that is the culmination of the entire *Argonautika*. First Medea rejuvenates Jason's father Aeson by killing and reviving him, but turning back time in the process, just as she has transformed a staff of olive wood back into an olive tree bearing fruit. Here the wooden artifact -- which is 'hylic' or material, like the Argo itself -- the static result of a process of experience or becoming, is traced back to the living process from which it has emerged. Next Medea does the same for the nurses of Dionysos, showing that the experience whose flow has nourished the psyche's differentiation can be the continuous

145

or eternal presence to it of the sources of its being. These two operations serve to establish Medea's capacities. In the final movement, involving Pelias and his daughters, Medea rejuvenates a dismembered ram, but leaves Pelias as his daughters -- generally with the exception of Alkestis -- have dismembered him.

The dismemberment of Pelias, like that of Apsyrtos, evokes Bacchic dismemberment, but that this fate should befall a son of Poseidon underscores an irreversibility to natural processes without which these would lack reality. In specific contrast to the ram's resurrection, Pelias proves all too mortal, and we must think that the logic of the myth attributes this, not to Medea's intention, which is merely part of the narrative frame, so to speak, but rather to the refusal of Alkestis to participate in a procedure that requires her to regard her father as a purely natural being, like the ram. Alkestis, for her part, features in another myth that, insofar as it has characters in common but a plot incompatible with the *Argonautika* episode, must be a parallel expression of the same logic. In the episode from the *Argonautika*, Alkestis refuses to slay her father, even if ostensibly to render him immortal, while in the other myth, she voluntarily enters the underworld to make her husband immortal after his parents have refused. The common element in the crossed structure of the two episodes is the power of Alkestis to grant immortality, but only at some unacceptable cost. Medea's operation, therefore, deploys simultaneously upon multiple planes of the divine, heroic and natural worlds, with different results on each level.

In a prolongation of the mythical dynamic that has driven the cycle, Medea's children by Jason are immortalized through being virtually sacrificed to Hera. Medea completes the cycle that began with Ixion by inverting Ixion's myth, winning the opportunity to immortalize her children by resisting Zeus's advances, hence refusing to create another heroic generation, a sun-king of Korinth who would unite the lines of Zeus and of Helios. Like a number of Hellenic myths, especially those which serve as the bases for tragic drama, this episode safeguards the proper life of the polis by voiding the position of joint holder of sacral and political power. Perhaps the most important occurrence of this motif is in the averted prophecy of Gaia and Ouranos regarding a son who would be born to Metis, who would become "king of Gods and humans" (Theogony 897). Medea's 'sacrifice' of a temporal sovereignty on Hera's behalf thus fulfills Hera's interest in the integrity of the political community. Medea becomes a Heraic life-giver for the Korinthian polis by exporting her own disruptive divinity with her trademark theatrical flourish of ascending dragons, rendering herself the extraordinary exception to its ordinary political life.

We have seen that the ideas with which the Platonists associate Hera can be grasped directly from her myths. The myths are not thus reduced to mere colorful illustrations of these ideas, for the myths are in reality immeasurably richer in content than the philosophical concepts. But neither are the concepts mere abstractions from theology; rather, they develop from their own parallel logic, which is an expression of divine activity as much as the myths are, neither more nor less direct an expression of the divine natures. Hera's myths are especially suited to augment the philosophical account of the emergence of psychical order in the cosmos, however, insofar as they treat particularly those phenomena which tend to obscure the clarity of philosophical perception to the very degree that they are also foundational for it: the negentropic 'vessels' of life, of sociality and political power, and the media of experience, the shapes of time and motion.

NOTES

[1] See, e.g., S. E. Gersh, *Kinesis Akinetos: A Study of Spiritual Motion in the Philosophy of Proclus* (Leiden: Brill, 1973).

[2] On this convergence generally, see Richard Seaford, "Dionysos as Destroyer of the Household: Homer, Tragedy, and the Polis," in Thomas H. Carpenter & Christopher A. Faraone, eds. *Masks of Dionysos* (Ithaca, NY: Cornell University Press, 1993), esp. 129-133.

[3] *Simplicius*, In Phys. 24, 17; trans. in Kirk, Raven & Schofield, eds. The Presocratic Philosophers, 2d ed. (Cambridge: Cambridge UP, 1983), 118.

[4] The fragments of Herakleitos are numbered according to Diels, while the translations are from Kirk, Raven and Schofield, The Presocratic Philosophers.

[5] Euripides, Medea 401-2 (Hugh Parry, Thelxis: Magic and Imagination in Greek Myth and Poetry (Lanham, MD: University Press of America, 1992), 134).

[6] "Language and Space: From Oedipus to Zola" in Hermes: Literature, Science, Philosophy ed. Harari and Bell (Baltimore, MD: Johns Hopkins, 1982), 48 (trans. mod.).

[7] Trans. Kirk, Raven and Schofield 1983, 195.

[8] Compare the interpretation of Odysseus as a primary figure of the Enlightenment subject in Horkheimer and Adorno's The Dialectic of Enlightenment.

[9] It is a principle, similarly, of Claude Lévi-Strauss's structural study of myth that all available variants of a myth are inseparable parts of it.

[10] Fr. 105 in Most 2007, 177.

HERA, MOTHER OF TYPHON:
THE PERILS OF GREEK VIRGIN BIRTH
by P. Sufenas Virius Lupus

Hera (or occasionally Juno) is said to have given birth to a variety of children in Greek and Roman myth, including Hebe, Eileithyia, the Charities, Ate, Eris, Ares, and Hephaistos.(1) On a few occasions, the latter two are said to have been borne by her without Zeus as their father, and were thus "virgin births." Hephaistos is said to have been such as early as Hesiod and the Homeric Hymn to Apollon (to be discussed below), as well as in several sources from late antiquity. Ares/Mars was said to have been engendered by Hera/Juno alone, with the help of a special flower from Flora, in Ovid's *Fasti* in his entry for the Flores on May 3rd, the final date of the games of the Floralia, thus explaining why Flora is so highly honored in the "city of Romulus" due to her role in the birth of Mars. (2)

However, a third child is said to have been the sole offspring of Hera in a virgin birth as well: Typhon. Typhon is also said to have been the child of Tartaros and Gaia, Tartaros and an otherwise unknown Tartara, or Gaia alone (again, by Ovid in Metamorphoses as well as by Vergil(3) and several others). The most extensive account of this is given in the *Homeric Hymn to Apollon.*

Near it there was a fair-flowing spring, where the lord,

son of Zeus, with his mighty bow, killed a she-dragon,

a great, glutted and fierce monster, which inflicted

many evils on the men of the land -- many on them

and many on their slender-shanked sheep; for she was
bloodthirsty.

149

And once from golden-throned Hera she received and reared

dreadful and baneful Typhaon, a scourge to mortals.

Hera once bore him in anger at father Zeus,

when indeed Kronides gave birth to glorious Athena

from his head; and mighty Hera was quickly angered

and spoke to the gathering of the immortal gods:

"All gods and all goddesses, hear from me

how cloud-gathering Zeus begins to dishonor me

first, since he made me his mindfully devoted wife,

and now apart from me gave birth to gray-eyed Athena,

who excels among all the blessed immortals.

But my son, Hephaistos, whom I myself bore

has grown to be weak-legged and lame among the blessed gods.

I took him with my own hands and cast him into the broad sea.

But Thetis, the silver-footed daughter of Nereus,

received him and with her sisters took him in her care.

I wish she had done the blessed gods some other favor!

O stubborn and wily one! What else will you now devise?

How dared you alone give birth to gray-eyed Athena?

Would not I have borne her? -- I, who was called your very own

among the immortals who dwell in the broad sky?

Take thought now, lest I devise some evil for you in return!

And now, I shall contrive to have born to me

a child who will excel among the immortals.

And to our sacred wedlock I shall bring no shame,

nor visit your bed, but I shall pass my time

far from you, among the immortal gods."

With these words she went apart from the gods very angry.

Then forthwith mighty, cow-eyed Hera prayed

and with the flat of her hand struck the ground and spoke:

"Hear me now, Earth and broad Sky above,

and you Titans from whom gods and men are descended

and who dwell beneath the earth round great Tartaros.

Hearken to me, all of you, and apart from Zeus grant me a child,

in no wise of inferior strength; nay, let him be stronger

than Zeus by as much as far-seeing Zeus is stronger than Kronos."

Then she cried out and lashed the earth with her stout hand.

Then the life-giving earth was moved and Hera saw it,

and her heart was delighted at the thought of fulfillment.

From then on, and until a full year came to its end,

she never came to the bed of contriving Zeus,

not pondered for him sagacious counsels,

sitting as before on her elaborate chair,

but staying in temples, where many pray,

cow-eyed, mighty Hera delighted in her offerings.

But when the months and the days reached their destined goal,

and the seasons arrived as the year revolved,

she bore dreadful and baneful Typhaon, a scourge to mortals,

whose aspect resembled neither god's nor man's.

Forthwith cow-eyed, might Hera took him and, piling evil

upon evil, she commended him to the care of the she-dragon.

He worked many evils on the glorious races of men,

and she brought their day of doom to those who met her,

until the lord far-shooting Apollon shot her

with a mighty arrow; rent with insufferable pains,

she lay panting fiercely and writhing on the ground.(4)

Perhaps, in this singular view in which Hera was the sole parent of Typhon, it is not merely his parentage and manner of conception which causes his evil nature, but also the fact that he was raised by the Drakaina Echidna/Python, who was also his future "wife" and the progenitor of many other monsters of Greek myth. Both "nature" in terms of his unusual conception, and "nurture" due to his contact with the Drakaina, may equally be the roots of Typhon's evil and destructive character.

Yet, further questions remain on these various virgin births of Hera/Juno. While it is likewise a minority interpretation that Ares/Mars was born without begetting by a male god, Ares/Mars is sometimes seen as the most "ungodly" of the principal gods in the traditional Olympian reckonings due to his warlike and even bestial nature. In Ovid's account, Hera gives birth to him in Thrace, that barbarian nation which most exemplified warlike excess to the Greeks. Likewise, in Ovid's account, it is over the upset at Zeus/Jupiter's giving birth to Athena/Minerva without a (visible) woman(5) that causes Hera/Juno to seek the answers she does from Flora. The same is said in the *Homeric Hymn to Apollon* in relation to Hera's virgin birth of Hephaistos. Hephaistos is additionally imperfect physically in comparison to his other divine siblings, no matter how talented he is in terms of his skill in artifice. Hephaistos' fosterage by Themis is considerably more fortunate than that of Typhon, certainly. Nonetheless, the imperfection of these virgin births from Hera alone is continued in this further example. Interestingly enough, both Hephaistos and Ares run afoul in various ways of Athena, their ostensibly elder sister born of Zeus, thus carrying the enmity of their mother into their own subsequent divine lives with similar resentments to their sister who was born from Zeus' head.

153

A theme thus emerges in these various female-only virgin births, which seems even amplified to some extent by inclusion of the Roman myths which cite Typhon as the sole offspring of the earth-goddess Gaia. Even when a deity as "manly" as Ares/Mars is concerned, it is deeply troubling to a male-dominated society to imagine that he could have emerged on female initiative alone, with no father as his rightful and recognized progenitor. The deep-seated patriarchal discomfort with the power of goddesses to generate offspring independent of male gods' insemination is reflected in these myths. Theologically, it is entirely neutral that a goddess (or, for that matter, a god!) could generate offspring independent of a mate of any possible gender; but socially, it is a very large problem that has much more to do with the gender norms and expectations of a given society than anything cosmologically significant.

That Typhon nearly destroys the order of the Olympian hegemonic godhead -- the celestial reflection of a well-ordered ancient Graeco-Roman society -- as a result of his generation by the will of a goddess acting alone says much more about the nature of the societies of the Hellenic (and later Roman) ancient Mediterranean than it does about the nature of these deities themselves. That other religions of late antiquity -- including various Gnostic beliefs (which saw Sophia generating without her male counterpart as the cause of the fallen and evil material world) concurred in this sort of thinking is noteworthy. However, a positive variation on some of these types of myth (including that of Christianity's virgin birth, even though a male godhead is still ultimately responsible there) could and did also exist. This suggests that modern understandings of these myths and deities could and should likewise adapt to the more egalitarian and attempted revisionist trends of the modern world in relation to the moral equality of the various genders. Perhaps Hera and her son Typhon can be re-envisioned and rehabilitated from centuries of misunderstanding and rejection in ways that are positive, and can suggest a closer and more equitable relationship between the human and divine communities and the unpredictable elemental forces of nature on the earth and in the wider cosmos.

Typhon as volcanic rumbler or dreadful storm, though still destructive and dangerous, need not be thought of as a force of evil bent on subversion of the rightful order of the cosmos, but instead as the danger inherent in allowing human stewardship of the earth to be without regard for the earth itself. Hera's forgotten and forsaken child may yet be a reminder for us all that the earth and the elements that compose it are deserving of respect and awe for their terrible and fearsome power, and that their wrath can be averted by more attention to responsible stewardship of the environment, and greater devotion to the gods and divine beings who dwell within those forces.

NOTES

1.   Vanessa James, *The Genealogy of Greek Mythology: An Illustrated Tree of Greek Myth from the First Gods to the Founders of Rome* (New York: Gotham Books/Melcher Media. Inc., 2003), pp. 15-16.

2.   Sir James George Frazer (ed./trans.), Ovid's *Fasti* (Cambridge: Harvard University Press, 1931), pp. 276-279; Lesley Adkins and Roy A. Adkins, Dictionary of Roman Religion (New York: Facts on File, 1996), pp. 80-81.

3.   H. Rushton Fairclough (ed./trans.), *Virgil, Volume One: Eclogues, Georgics, Aeneid I-VI* (Cambridge: Harvard University Press, 1950), pp. 100-101; Frank Justus Miller (ed./trans.), Ovid, Metamorphoses, Books I-VIII (Cambridge: Harvard University Press, 1999), pp. 260-261.

4. Apostolos N. Athanassakis, *The Homeric Hymns* (Baltimore and London: The Johns Hopkins University Press, 2004), pp. 24-25.

5. For more on Zeus' singular births, see P. Sufenas Virius Lupus, "An Obstetrician's Nightmare: Zeus and Male Birth," in Melia Suez et al. (eds.), *From Cave to Sky: A Devotional Anthology for Zeus* (Shreveport: Bibliotheca Alexandrina, 2010), pp. 42-55.

"SHREWISH PRINCESS"?:
DIVA SABINA AUGUSTA AND THE
HERA/JUNO SYNCRETISM

by P. Sufenas Virius Lupus

Due to the syncretism -- both before his death and afterwards -- of the Divine Emperor Hadrian to Zeus,(1) it might seem obvious that it would be likely, therefore, that his wife (who predeceased him), Diva Vibia Sabina Augusta, would therefore be syncretized as well to Hera. Hadrian's completion of the temple of Zeus Olympeios in Athens(2) forever cemented his connection to that deity, but likewise Hadrian's benefactions for the goddess Hera are also known from antiquity. He is responsible for the foundation of the temple of Hera in Athens(3) as well as that of Zeus. Pausanias also notes that Hadrian's gifts to a temple of Hera about two miles from Mycenae included a gold, jewel-encrusted peacock.(4)

Therefore, it would seem that the syncretism of Diva Sabina to Hera would make sense on a variety of levels. But, at the same time, one should ask whether it truly does or not, and whether the mythological character of Hera and her jealous relationship to Zeus has been over-read into the relationship between the Empress Sabina and her husband Hadrian. While the evidence for the syncretism of Hera to Diva Sabina does certainly exist, as will be discussed presently, the question of how this evidence has been overestimated needs to be addressed as well.

Of first priority in the present discussion, therefore, is the giving of details on the ancient evidence for the syncretism of Diva Sabina Augusta to Hera. Diva Sabina is also visually syncretized to Venus and Ceres, and is even called the "New Demeter" on one occasion.(5) Thorsten Opper comments, "Cities around the empire erected statues in [Sabina's] honour, usually in conjunction with those for Hadrian and sometimes in the guise of goddesses such as Juno, Venus and Ceres."(6) At present, I know of one instance in which Diva Sabina receives the epithet "New Hera" on an altar from the Greek island of Thasos.(7) At Antinoöpolis, the city founded in honor of Antinous at the spot in Egypt where he drowned in the Nile, a phyla (administrative district) is named for Sabina, and the deme- ("tribe") names under her phyla include Heraieus, "Hera-like."(8) While my knowledge of this subject is not as comprehensive as I'd like it to be, and all of the available sources are not easily obtained, nonetheless the evidence for this syncretism is less common or widespread than one might infer from Opper's comments.(9)

Very little is known about the life and personality of Diva Sabina Augusta, and while this does not make her much different from many of the other imperial wives and relatives around Hadrian, as well as other Emperors, who became Divae after their deaths, nonetheless I suspect that the syncretism of Diva Sabina to Hera has been used to "fill in the blanks" on her personality in certain respects. The historiographic tendency to see this syncretism as in some way definitive of the actual relationship of Diva Sabina to Hadrian is a bit problematic, but is supported by the information in such ancient sources as the *Historia Augusta*. This source has very little to say on Diva Sabina in its life of Hadrian, other than the following two passages.

Septicius Clarus, prefect of the guard, and Suetonius Tranquillus, director of his correspondence, he replaced, because they had at that time behaved in the company of his wife Sabina, in their association with her, in a more informal fashion than respect for the court household demanded. He would have dismissed his wife, too, for being moody and difficult -- if he had been a private citizen, as [Hadrian] himself used to say.(10)

158

At this time indeed, Sabina his wife died, not without a rumour that poison had been given her by Hadrian.(11)

Remarks attributed to her in the *Epitome de Caesaribus* also suggest that she did everything in her power to prevent a viable pregnancy engendered by Hadrian.(12) However, these types of statement, scant though they are, have been over-read due to their rarity in a rather poor exercise of logical positivism (i.e. that the only evidence we have for something must be the only matters which are taken seriously), despite the fact that the sources concerned are late and demonstrably biased. Opper prudently expresses reservation on these matters.

> While these passages make entertaining reading, it is hard to assess their veracity. Her marriage to Hadrian, if ever consummated, certainly remained childless. However, the descriptions of Hadrian's behavior towards Sabina were clearly designed to contrast with his reported treatment of Antinous, and this dichotomy, and Sabina's reaction to that relationship, have very much intrigued all modern commentators. Whatever the truth may have been, the Roman public's perception of the first couple is likely to have been very different. In the official court ritual and the public representation of the imperial family Hadrian treated Sabina in the same respectful manner with which Trajan had treated his female relatives before him.(13)

Diva Sabina's inferred opinions on Antinous(14) are very likely out of association of the syncretisms of Diva Sabina to Hera, Hadrian to Zeus, and Antinous to Ganymede. Indeed, later in the first passage quoted from the *Historia Augusta* above, both philandering and homoerotic relationships with adult males are attributed to Hadrian,(15) just as they would have been to Zeus, which suggests that this historiographic reading of the real-life characters of the Emperor and his Empress were already being done along literalizing allegorical lines suggested by mythology in late antiquity.

159

It is also possible that this line of reasoning also occurs in one of Lukian of Samosata's Dialogues of the Gods between Hera and Zeus, where Hera's main complaint is that she is being left in the cold now that Ganymede has been brought to Olympus.(16) As in other works of Lukian, Zeus is implied to stand for Hadrian and Ganymede for Antinous, as Lukian was a critic of the cultus of Antinous.(17) It should be noted that the syncretism of Antinous to Ganymede, while it is "obvious" and implied by many modern commentators and historians in relation to the cultus of Antinous, was in fact never attested in the ancient cultus itself, outside of critics like Lukian and the various Christian authors who were against its existence.(18)

In the absence of any of Diva Sabina Augusta's actual words, on herself or on Antinous, and lacking the survival of Hadrian's autobiography, we can never really know for certain what the truths of these matters are. The only two beings prayed for by Antinous who are named on the Obelisk of Antinous -- arguably, the most important relic from his ancient cultus to partially survive -- are Hadrian and Sabina.(19) One of the few apotheosis reliefs to survive from the Roman Imperial Period is one showing Hadrian and Diva Sabina being carried aloft by the Imperial Iuno, the feminine counterpart to the Imperial Genius.(20) These facts alone suggest that modern devotees of Antinous and Hadrian should give the benefit of the doubt to Diva Sabina Augusta, and should honor her as the rightful wife and exemplar of feminine virtue and divinity amongst the various human and divine members of the Antinoan pantheon.

Therefore, it may be more useful to think of the relationship of Hadrian and Diva Sabina in more positive terms. The Capitoline Triad in the later periods of Roman history consisted of Jupiter, Juno, and Minerva,(21) with no indications that there was any ill feeling between one member of this triad and another. In fact, Hadrian, Sabina, and Antinous could form a triad of their own which corresponds to the Capitoline Triad for modern devotees of these deified mortals.

Mythology, and the academic commentators upon it, paint Hera as a shrewish wife, but there is no need therefore to assume that Diva Sabina Augusta was likewise a "shrewish princess" in terms of her marriage to Hadrian. But, a wider point is also possible to infer from this re-envisioning of Hera and Diva Sabina in terms of the cultic realities of the Roman goddess Juno. We need not view Hera as simply characterized by shrewishness, jealousy, and anger over her husband's extra-marital affairs. The scene in the Iliad which depicts Hera's consummation of her marriage with Zeus, after all of his other dalliances with other goddesses have already occurred,(22) is a beautiful scene, despite being a distraction which Hera contrives in order to take attention away from Zeus' overseeing the Trojan War.

> At that the son of Cronos clasped his wife in his arms, and beneath them the bright earth made fresh-sprung grass to grow, and dewy lotus, and crocus, and hyacinth thick and soft that kept them from the ground. On this they lay, and were clothed with a cloud, fair and golden, from which fell drops of glistening dew.(23)

It bears mentioning that the red Nile lotus ended up being named after Antinous after his death and apotheosis, and in this passage from the Iliad, though the red Nile lotus is not specified, the coincidence of these flower types is noteworthy.(24) The crocus and the hyacinth, likewise, were flowers that grew up as a result of the death of a homoerotic beloved in Greek myth. It would be a potentially beautiful and inspiring image to adopt the red Nile lotus of Antinous sprouting up to support the marriage-bed of Diva Sabina and Hadrian, whose union as the earthly embodiments of the great goddess and god, Hera and Zeus in their just and rightful rule of the cosmos, is the force upon the earth and amongst humanity that allows the grass to grow.

NOTES

1. "Roman Olympians: The Cult of Zeus and Hadrian Olympios," in *From Cave to Sky: A Devotional Anthology for Zeus* (Bibliotheca Alexandrina, 2010), pp. 97-105.

2. Ibid.

3. Thorsten Opper, *Hadrian: Empire and Conflict* (Cambridge: Harvard University Press, 2008), p. 128.

4. Anthony R. Birley, *Hadrian: The Restless Emperor* (London and New York: Routledge, 2000), p. 178.

5. Ibid.

6. Opper, p. 203. I have not been able to consult the sources listed in Opper's bibliography on this point at present.

7. Anna S. Benjamin, "The Altars of Hadrian in Athens and Hadrian's Panhellenic Program," *Hesperia 32.1* (January-March 1963), pp. 57-86 at 77 §139.

8. P. Sufenas Virius Lupus, Devotio Antinoo: *The Doctor's Notes, Volume One* (The Red Lotus Library, 2011), pp. 399-400.

9. As reported by Birley, Hadrian, p. 178, Sabina also had a statue at Hermione near Troezen; and likewise Simon R. F. Price, *Rituals and Power: The Roman Imperial Cult in Asia Minor* (Cambridge: Cambridge University Press, 1986), p. 273 §146, mentions an imperial temple with statues of Vespasian, Titus, Nerva, Trajan, Hadrian, and Sabina. Both of these locations would seem likely places in which an inscription or statuary attribute might connect Diva Sabina with Hera, but the sources above do not indicate such.

10. Anthony R. Birley, *Lives of the Later Caesars: The first part of the Augustan History*, with newly compiled Lives of Nerva and Trajan (London and New York: Penguin Books, 1976), p. 69.

11. Birley, Lives, p. 83.

12. Opper, p. 203.

13. Ibid.

14. As witnessed in, e.g., Elizabeth Speller, *Following Hadrian: A Second-century Journey through the Roman Empire* (London: Review/Headline Book Publishing, 2002). It should also be noted that the Emperor and Empress' visit to the Colossoi of Memnon a few weeks after the death of Antinous in Egypt, and the records of their visit left on the statue, show no signs of acknowledgement of Antinous' death, which has been taken as a sign that the Empress was indifferent or antagonistic to his deification and his relationship to Hadrian; however, the one inscription by Diva Sabina herself is obliterated before it goes on to say anything. For these inscriptions, see Lupus, Devotio, pp. 342-346.

15. Birley, Lives, p. 69.

16. M. D. MacLeod (ed./ trans.), *Lucian, Volume VII* (Cambridge: Harvard University Press, 1961). pp. 268-275.

17. P. Sufenas Virius Lupus, *A Garland for Polydeukion* (The Red Lotus Library, 2012), pp. 109-120.

18. P. Sufenas Virius Lupus, *The Syncretisms of Antinous* (The Red Lotus Library, 2010), pp. 113-119.

19. Lupus, Devotio, p. 352.

20. Birley, Hadrian, pp. 293-294.

21. Lesley Adkins and Roy A. Adkins, *Dictionary of Roman Religion* (New York: Facts on File, 1996), p. 39.

22. A. T. Murray (ed./trans.), Homer, *Iliad*, Books 13-24, revised by Willaim F. Wyatt (Cambridge: Harvard University Press, 2001), pp. 78-93.

23. Murray, pp. 92-93.

24. Indeed, in vase paintings, Hera is shown holding a scepter topped with a lotus; see

http://www.theoi.com/Gallery/K4.1.html.

ON THE ORPHIC HYMN TO HERA
by Lykeia

Editor's Note: see Appendix A for translations of the Orphic Hymn to Hera by Apostolos N. Athanassakis and Thomas Taylor.

The Orphic Hymn to Hera is of value because it illuminates the nature of Hera, outside of myth, within the world and cosmos. It is also valuable as it demonstrates the material parallel of Hera's domain with that of her spouse Zeus. Just as he is of the aetheric domain -- and thus all things of our world by this nature are connected to him by his energy that surrounds and is within them -- so Hera in her hymn is described as airy, the very material substance which ensconces all things and upon which all life depends as we draw it within our bodies. Socrates appears to agree with this interpretation of Hera's name as Plato records in his Cratylus.

> "But perhaps the rule-setter, being a lofty thinker, called her 'Hera' as a disguised name for air, putting the end of her name at the beginning -- you'll get the idea if you repeat the name 'Hera' over and over."(1)

In this fashion we find that Hera's (pronounced 'Era) name is fluid and ever flowing like that nature of air itself, with the ending at once the beginning again of her name, without distinction of a beginning or ending within her. As the daughter of Rhea this makes sense as we find that, earlier in the text, Socrates speaks of Rhea and the name of Kronos as being derived from ideas pertaining to streams; eg Rhea is from rhoe, the flowing of a river. As the heir of Rhea, it is perhaps natural that Hera's nature too is that of a flowing kind. That which is constant but never fixed, for as Socrates says, "you cannot step into the same river twice."(2)

165

It is by this nature that Hera is mutable, and rather difficult to clearly see manifest, unlike those gods who have very clear visible signs of their domain reflected in the natural world (eg, the light of Apollon and Artemis, the fricative seas of Poseidon, the fertile earth and grain of Demeter, the hearth and altar of Hestia and so forth). In comparison, Hera is beyond our sight, even as we cannot visually perceived the air. We may see vapor, or the movement of debris during a windy day, or the movement of clouds. But air, which is a recognized necessity to life, we cannot see even as we partake of it and are sustained by it (unless, in a sense, when viewing the ozone from space). Thus even if we do not readily discern the presence of Hera, she is necessarily there with us. It seems it is in this vein that we find the opening of the Orphic Hymn in the Athanassakis translation speaking of the goddess as being ensconced in darksome hollows and attributed to possessing an airy form. However, in his translation of the hymn Thomas Taylor does not make any mention of this other than saying in his second line that she is "aerial-formed". He may allude to it vaguely in saying that she is enthroned in the blue air, which has a typically homogenous appearance surrounding the earth in which no particular element within it could be identified as being a fixed point of praise to her, but rather than she is everywhere all around, otherwise indiscernible, concealed in this "blue throne." This is particularly evident if one ever visits Montana and experiences "big sky country" in person.

It is perhaps reasonable that this occurs within the opening lines of both translations, where she is also affirmed to be Queen, and to be the wife of Zeus. This serves as a reminder that she is of the highest order and her domain is on par with that of Zeus, and possessing a parallel nature to his aetheric nature that contains all. So while Zeus is by nature the father of all life, she too is by nature the mother of all life. This can be supplemented by the Homeric Hymn to Hera in which she is praised as one to whom all the gods pay reverence, even as they pray it to Zeus. Athanassakis goes so far to address the breezes with which she brings relief to mortals while simultaneously nourishing the soul, whereas Taylor has a rather convoluted line that she nurture's life "which every life desires." I would take this strange wording to imply that a life which every life desires is a life that is both tangible by its nature of being a living being but also one that is internal, and thus something possible to be desired by the living; eg, the common phrase "I/You need to get a life." Thus, by understanding that the model of the soul is a microcosm of the world, those effects that Hera brings to her domain in the natural world around us are also taking affect within the soul, causing a beneficial movement within the soul that aids in its growth.

This can be further developed in Athanassakis' translation, which describes her as one who nurtures the winds; it is through her that the winds that allow movement are made possible. Alternatively, Taylor in his translation addresses her as the mother of the winds and clouds, making these as things that are causing action which are produced through her. The movement of (unpredictable) winds would have been vitality important to a sea-faring people; equally important was the winds' more fearsome form of storms, and here we find Hera addressed as Telkhinia. It is perhaps more beneficial to see Telkhinia as being addressed for good winds by sailors, and as such we too would desire her good winds to carry our souls forward. That she was offered a black lamb in sacrifice on the Areopagos in Athens within days of the holocaust to Zeus Epoptes ("the overseer") may also have some ramifications on the vital, if not always pleasant, functions of Hera Telkhinia; eg, as a maternal goddess of the autumn rains and storms at the end of the month Metageitnon, following the harvest season, and the sacrifice of Persephone associated with this time of the year in the Greater Mysteries.(3)

This beneficial movement brings with it blessings. In both translations we find the blessings materializing as rain, although rather indirectly with Taylor: he calls her the mother of clouds, which is often symbolized by the herald of the cuckoo bird who brings the spring rains. In this fashion, as the cuckoo is the herald of Hera but is also in myth described as a form taken by Zeus, we can understand that the appearance of the bird and the arrival of rain is from a cooperative act of love between them. The necessity of love between Zeus and Hera and its relevancy in the world can be inferred by the first translation Socrates gives of Hera's name as "lovable." The marriage of Zeus and Hera is often celebrated during the rainy season of late winter; as such, we can certainly view the return of fertility, the appearance of new green life, all from the rain, in relation to the creative action of Zeus and Hera together. This generative nature that is symbolized with the rain represents that which creates physical biological life, and that which is formative on the soul's life. It is then easy to see why Taylor's translation follows with a declaration that all things share Hera's temperament, for she, like Zeus, is within all things; and Athanassakis' translation states that she takes partakes in all things, even as she is mixed through the air; it is thus implied that we partake in her, too, just as we partake of the air.

It is the last lines of the hymn that we are given the impression of her great power as Hera Telkinia, which was briefly spoken of earlier, as one who produces great storms through the winds and seas. Taylor says that it is through her that there are great blasts of winds from which the seas swell, which certainly implies a certain relationship with Poseidon; that relationship can be illuminated further from the myth in which Hera persuaded Poseidon to restore to sea to the shores of Argos. Additionally, she her stormy nature causes the rivers to roar fiercely and flood. This fierce power, which so violently alters the environment, but in ultimately beneficially ways (fertile new soil is washed up onto the ground), can destroy lives as much as bring new life. It is in this context we can understand Hera as the maker of heroes, as a goddess who roars with raging winds that seem to threaten all hope of success or life, but which results ultimately in goodly things even if it doesn't seem so at the time. Thus, Taylor invites her as a goddess who is kind, rejoicing and serene, while Athanassakis invites her to come with kindness and joy on her lovely face;

these evoke a goddess of great compassion, love and benevolence, and these qualities compose a good part of the unsurpassing beauty she is described as having in her Homeric Hymn.

"O Royal Juno of majestic mien,

Aerial-formed, divine, Jove's blessed queen,

Thron'd in the bosom of caerulean air,

The race of mortals is thy constant care.

The cooling gales thy pow'r alone inspires,

Which nourish life, which ev'ry life desires.

Mother of clouds and winds, from thee alone

Producing all things, mortal life is known:

All natures share thy temp'rament divine,

And universal sway alone is thine.

With founding blasts of wind, the swelling sea

And rolling rivers roar, when shook by thee.

Come, blessed Goddess, fam'd almighty queen,

With aspect kind, rejoicing and serene." (4)

NOTES:

1 Plato, "Cratylus," Plato: Complete Works; John M. Cooper Editor; 404C

2 Plato 402A

3 Diodorus Siculus, *Library of History* 5.55.5; Parker, Robert. *Polytheism and Society at Athens*, Oxford University Press, NY (2005): pg 68 footnote 68.

4 *Orphic Hymn 76* Translated by Thomas Taylor

HERA:
A GNOSTIC-CHRISTIAN VIEW
OF THE GODDESS
by Robert F. Koenig

Editor's Note: the following essay examines Hera from a Gnostic Christian perspective. As such, it draws primarily from non-Greek sources for information and inspiration, most notably the Biblical Wisdom texts, the Kabbalah, Christian Apocrypha, and ancient beliefs and practices centered on the Virgin Mary.

How does one look into a connection between the Hellenic Goddess and Christianity? Not easily, but such connections are there if you look for them. It is the purpose of this article to highlight some possible connections between Hera and the Bible.

I, myself, had been a lifelong Christian, dabbling in other books here and there, even trying out a few different styles of religion. I have had many visions in dreams over the past couple of years. Hermes appeared in one dream, handed me a letter, and said he had a message for me -- yet I never actually opened the contents. Or was this Hermes' way to inviting me to a calling? Another dream placed me in a sacred marriage ceremony, where I was becoming connected to the Goddess. The cup of Hera was before me, and I was the blade. Did she ask me to be Her advocate, or devotee? Even Her priest? Since that powerful dream, a crimson haired beauty has twice appeared in my visions.

We Gnostics define ourselves as learning, or coming to know, mystical or intellectual knowledge, combining both Christian and Pagan ideas. In my search for the divine feminine, I felt that She in turn, in dreams, gave me inner knowledge. I came away from such dreams feeling a connection to Hera, which led me to examine available knowledge about her.

In my research I discovered that Hera, whom the Greeks billed as "the Queen of the Gods," is the least respected deity today. Some ancient vases show Hera standing proud (with Zeus seemingly puzzled at this display of power), and at least one cult addressed him as "Hera's Zeus." Today, though, Greek Goddesses such as Athena, Aphrodite, Artemis, and Demeter have plenty of followers and books devoted to them. Hera, though, is known as the "jealous" wife. Zeus tends to play the field, having children with human women, and even some of Hera's own sisters. She is the Goddess of Marriage, and June (named for her Roman equivalent Juno) remains a popular month for weddings. In the myths, Hera seems to be best known for dooming Zeus' conquests, or attacking their progeny. How can a Goddess of marriage have such a horrible coupling? Certainly not a becoming lifestyle for the Queen!

Patricia Monaghan, author of The Goddess Path, reveals how Hera may have been made less powerful by joining with another pantheon:

> I love Hera! One of my matron goddesses. You should look into the pre-Hellenic Hera, who was a goddess much more solitary than the later one, who was 'married' to Zeus as a means of 'converting' her people."(1)

Monaghan was correct, according to Anne Baring and Jules Cashford in The Myth of The Goddess:

> The mythic defeat of the Mother Goddess by a God is not, of course, unique to Babylonian mythology or to the Old Testament, but is enacted in the myths of every culture where the new rule of sky-gods is super-imposed on the older Goddess religion.(2)

How was Hera primordially a powerful Goddess, and what were Her origins? Some possibilities can be found within the books of the Bible itself! Goddess worship was more profound than God worship in that the Female actually brought forth life. Excavations of ancient ruins have produced many a statue in the form of a female. In early Canaan God was El, and his wife was Asherah, who was often worshipped as a tree. Asherah is mentioned in the Bible forty times, but not always in a positive manner. Many parts of the Bible seem to hide anything about the Mother Goddess, and there is scant little information about the women who travelled with His son, Jesus. In Proverbs we learn of the Feminine Sophia, the personified Wisdom who was with God before creation. While she is seen as the Holy Spirit by some, most Christian sects ignore Her. And while Jesus' mother, the Virgin Mary, and Mary Magdalene, are discussed in countless research, very little is written about them in the actual Bible. When I asked fellow Gnostic, Zeke Li, about Goddesses in the Bible he offered this reply:

> Around 1200 and 1800 B.C., the God is a form of Zeus and El, while His consort is Hera and Asherah/Eloah. This is why Hera is also called Ash-hera. Both Asherah in the Book of Jeremiah and the Greco-Roman times Hera bore the epithet "Queen of Heaven."(3)

In the Bible, King Solomon builds a temple for Wisdom. Sophia, in many ways the hidden Goddess of the gospels, was God's first creation, and his consort during creation. Many see Her as the Holy Ghost, as "Asher" (somewhat an abbreviation of Asherah) is also a name for the Holy Spirit, and connected with the tree of life in Kabbalah; this makes the divine family Father (God/Yahweh), Mother (Sophia/Wisdom) and son (Jesus/Yeshua/Logos). Is there a three part family in Hera's life? We shall discuss this further below.

Looking deeper into the Bible, a theme seems to arise. God is seen as a brash, jealous God in the Old Testament. He punishes (floods, pestilence), is seen as a burning bush, and is heard in loud thunder. Could you not see this role being that of Zeus? The Wisdom Books (Song Of Solomon, Wisdom, Proverbs) reveal to us that Wisdom is a being, and She was there at the beginning of creation. Proverbs 8:29 reads: "When He fixed the foundations of the Earth, then I was beside Him as artisan."(4) Surely this sounds like a divine couple, weaving a galaxy together.

Next, we go to the New Testament. The Old Testament mentions a Messiah who would be born unto the world, and

Mary, through the Holy Spirit, would bear Jesus. The Apocryphal Book of Philip questions how the Spirit, who is female, can make Mary with child. Some suggest Mary is the Divine Mother made flesh, while Jesus is the Divine Father come into the world. Jesus, although the Son of God, is actually discussed in a lecture through Gnostic Radio as the "Jew-Zeus."(5)

As Divine Queen of Heaven, Hera is also connected to the Virgin Mary. Mary is often titled as Mother of God, or Queen of Heaven. Hera is oft addressed as "Lady." With the many sightings and visions of the Virgin Mary, the "Mother of God" is called by many titles, most starting with "Our Lady." A few of her many titles are:

Our Lady of Fatima
Our Lady Of Grace
Our Lady of Guadeloupe
Our lady Of Charity
Our Lady of the Immaculate Conception
Our Lady of Lourdes
Our Lady Of Mercy
Our Lady of the Miraculous Medal
Our Lady Of Hope
Our Lady Of Regla

Interestingly, many of Mary's titles are included in prayers for fertility, family, and the fidelity of marriage. Of course, marriage and childbirth are Hera's areas of interest. Hera was also seen wearing a crown of stars, and Mary is usually pictured adorned with stars around her head. And, once a year, Hera bathes in the river Imbrasus to renew her virginity. Mary is sometimes called "Maria Regina," thus connecting her to Hera's Roman counterpart Juno who was also titled "Regina."

Artistic depictions of Hera show her in many different ways; for instance, with Her wisdom and beauty, enthroned and surrounded by peacocks. I personally see Hera with hair of red. The young Virgin Mary, as described by visionary Anne

Catherine Emmerich, when entering the Temple as a child, had "reddish fair-hair, curling at the ends."(6)   Consider the symbolism of Hera's red hair: scarlet, the red of rage, the loving and gentle Goddess of Marriage's reaction to a cheating husband.

Returning to the idea of a three-part family surrounding Hera, let us consider the figure of Heracles. Not considered born of Hera, Heracles is rather son of Zeus and the human woman Alcmene. Given Hera's hatred over Zeus' follies, it is interesting that this child is named after her: Heracles means "Glory Of Hera," as if to make it seem that she would be proud to claim a son such as this. Hera, who usually attacked Zeus' progeny and girlfriends, also attempted to kill the infant Heracles with snakes in his crib, which he defeated. Hera was later tricked(?) into suckling the child. He apparently sucked so hard, that when she brushed him away, her milk shot into the sky, creating the Milky Way! This makes me think of Sophia being at God's side during the creation of our galaxy.   Half-human and half-immortal, the adult Heracles was sent to complete twelve labors to gain full immortality and join the Olympians.   The number twelve makes one think of Jesus' twelve disciples, the twelve signs of the zodiac, or even the twelve months of the year.

These stories are myths and teach something, but they also have a ring of truth behind them. If Hera was not Heracles' mother, and his mother was human, than he has yet another connection to Jesus. Connecting the families together, we could have:

Father: God/Zeus
Mother: Mary-Sophia/Hera
Son: Jesus/ Heracles

To support this theory further, consider the Lord's Prayer, which comes with this ending in most Christian sects:

For Thine Is The Kingdom,
And The Power,
And The Glory,
Forever And Ever, Amen.

Zeus has the Kingdom. Mount Olympus is his abode. This is known. Heracles, as the "glory" of Hera, receives his title. In another myth, Hera offered power to the Trojan prince, Paris; eg lordship of Europe and Asia. Athena offered wisdom, and Aphrodite offered the most beautiful woman alive. Paris chose Aphrodite's gift, and was given Helen of Troy. This tale became the basis for the Trojan War. Thus, all three gifts -- a kingdom, power, and glory -- which appear in the ending of the Lord's Prayer also appear in the tale of Paris.

Now, having established a theory as to Hera's origins, let us consider what her name truly means. First, we can look into the meaning of the name of God. In Hebrew, God is Yahweh. Or, in four letters , YHWH. Or, in the Kabbalistic alphabet, Yod-Hei-Vav-Hei. Yod, the first letter, represents the Father, God. Hei is Feminine and represents the Divine Mother. Vav, or Jahovah, is God the Son, or Jesus. The Second Hei can be a Divine Daughter. This suggests a Divine Tetragrammaton of Father-Mother-Son-Daughter.

Thus, we see the possibility of a piece of Hera's name. If one pronounces it as Hei-ra, Her aspect as a Divine Mother stands true.

The other piece of Hera's name -- ra -- may come from both a Biblical and Egyptian past. Ra, an Egyptian God, was also Egypt's solar deity. (Some suggest Jesus was a solar deity as well.) Ra has some similarities in the myths to Hera. Ra ruled the sky, and was associated with hawks. In a myth of Ra, cows are in play; Hera is referred as a Cow-Eyed Goddess, perhaps to connect her to the Goddess Io, one of Zeus' conquests who also has connections to Egypt and the Goddess Isis. Ra's cult grew in Heliopolis, known as the "Place of Pillars" to Egyptians. In the

Old Testament, Sophia built Her house with seven "columns" (Proverbs 9:1) which could be very easily read as "pillars."

Eyes also play a role in Hera's myths. Her sacred animal, the peacock, is known for the males of the species having beautiful, elongated tail feathers. These feathers have spots, or "eyes" at the end of each feather. In one myth, Hera's herdsman Argus has a thousand eyes. She sets him to guard Io after Hera has transformed the latter into a cow. Argus was killed, though, and, in tribute, Hera placed his eyes into the feathers of her favorite animal. Thus is her symbol and favorite animal all-seeing.

In short, placing together Hei, the Divine Feminine in the Kabbalistic/Hebrew alphabet with Ra creates Hera -- the all-seeing, all-knowing Divine Queen of Heaven!

Crowned and regal, Hera has been ignored and belittled for too long. Our culture should cherish Hera during June. Does Hera exist? We should accept the Gods/Goddesses in all the forms in which they appear before us.

Praise Hera!!

Notes:
1: Patricia Monaghan. Facebook discussion, 2012.
2: Baring, Anne and Cashford, Jules. *The Myth of the Goddess: Evolution of an Image*. Viking Arkana/Penguin Books, New York, 1991. Pg 420.
3: Zeke Li. Facebook discussion, 2012.
4: *The New American Bible*, Catholic Book Publishing Corp. New Jersey. Pg 737.
5: http://gnosticradio.org/lectures/lectures-by-topic/bible/243-yeshua-the-jew-zeus/view-details
6: Emmerich, Anne Catherine. *The Life Of The Blessed Virgin Mary*. Tan Books, North Carolina, 1954. Pg 88.

"ALTAR"
by Lykeia

EVLÁVEIA

A MODERN WORSHIP OF HERA
by Lykeia

Of all the goddesses honored in modern times, it seems a bit surprising that Hera doesn't get much love, when in fact she is one of the more important goddesses. At most, one may see a pendulum swinging in extremes one way or the other. Hera has been portrayed as the equivalent of the evil stepmother; her jealousies against the children of her spouse are typical of the ominous relationship between stepchildren and the stepmother who wants to displace them with her own children. Alternatively, there is also the feminist support for Hera, which vilifies Zeus and asserts that Hera is a displaced queen goddess who is more or less in an abusive and unwanted relationship. In the end it seems that both of these modern interpretations draw from a literal interpretation of the myths surrounding Hera and her relationship with Zeus, and they tend to be out of sync with the historic worship of the goddess. This "out of syncness" could be repaired with an allegorical view of the same myths.

Having an allegorical perspective on the myths also solves some of their more seemingly contradictory elements. For instance, if Hera so reviled Herakles, then why does his name mean "Glory of Hera"? The myth of Herakles is perhaps one of the most complicated of relationships between Hera and one of her husband's mortal offspring. This complexity, while oftentimes seeming harsh and demanding, comes with trials that elevate the mortal being. Through the trials of Hera, Herakles was able to not only join the gods, but also join in marriage with her daughter, Hebe. Plato says that the children of Zeus are of the quality of kings; with this in mind, Hera takes the strong hand that is necessary to temper the fine metal of these children to make even the most headstrong among them a great leader or hero. Thus, even as Zeus and Hera are linked throughout their cosmic and divine domains, so too they are linked here, through the creation and inspiration of greatness. I consider this to be a far more preferable platform to build on to that of the abused or abusive wife.

Considering that the marriage between Zeus and Hera is necessary and essential to the life of the world and cosmos, it is logical if one's domestic worship of Hera includes a shared shrine and service of prayers to Hera and Zeus together. Although I have never found any evidence of a domestic name and function of Hera, it seems reasonable to my mind that she would have been honored with her spouse within the household; as such, in my own household, they have long shared a shrine. On that shrine sits one of my favorite paintings, "Jupiter and Juno on Mt Ida" by James Barry, alongside a sprig of olive from Olympia where Zeus and Hera historically had great temples established. I chose this image because, of all the images of Zeus and Hera, it conveys to me the essential closeness of the gods: entwined in each others' embrace, they look into each other's eyes. The dance of the material goddess Hera, queen of the earth, airy one, and the aetheric Zeus, he who produces light, bringer of clouds that nourish the earth with rain, makes an appropriate focus for establishing a shrine for Hera if one worships her alongside her kingly spouse. (Of course, Hera can be -- and from what I can tell, often is -- worshiped singularly on her own shrine, surrounded by all the beauty of her sacred symbols.) That said, it is not improbable for a household to have multiple shrines honoring the same gods in different ways. One may have a main shrine to Hera, and then have smaller pair shrines of the goddess with gods to establish different foci of emphasis for the blessings that the goddess brings to the household: for instance, Athena, Artemis, Eileithyia, Apollon, Aphrodite, Hephaistos, and Poseidon.

When sharing a shrine with Zeus, for instance, it would not be odd to see Athena among them also, with whom Hera shares a special relationship, despite her mythic anger at Zeus' singular delivery of that goddess. Though we see this a bit less commonly in Hellenic art and temples, it seems that this triad was particularly appreciated by the Romans: quite probably

181

influenced by the relationship of the three gods in the Hellenic world, they erected numerous temples to Jupiter, Juno and Minerva throughout their empire. Not only did Athena and Hera in one myth conspire with Poseidon in a brief rebellion against Zeus, but we find them also in close alliance with each other in the Iliad with Hera acting as Athena's charioteer. Acting together, the goddesses provide an overwhelmingly powerful front against their enemies, even against mighty Ares. In a modern context, worship of Hera and Athena together is beneficial for fortitude and stability of one's oikos, as well as the overall care and well being of the family. A child, or individual, may also benefit from having this triad in their personal room, that worship given there may inspire great temperance and strength of will and character.

Perhaps it is with similar purpose that we find the Ionian triad of Zeus, Hera and Artemis together. In this case, Artemis displays powerfully protective roles and militaristic functions, in addition to also being the divine nurse who supports the rule of Zeus and Hera not only by her aggressive nature, but also by her nurturing functions. Worshipped in such a triad, the focus can shift to the genitive continuation of the oikos: Zeus and Hera's domains of the procreative substances in action within the oikos are supported by the protective nurse/huntress who urges the young to new and higher growth and development. Such a triad would be well worshiped in the family common room; or, especially for babies and very small children, in their bedrooms to provide care and protection for the new generations of the oikos.

In the context of worship in Thrake and Krete, this paired association between Hera and Artemis would make even greater sense as Artemis is considered in both places to be a daughter of Hera. Unlike mainland Hellas, Krete established Hera as mother of most of the Olympian deities, making Hera a mother goddess figure to a far greater extant than she may have been elsewhere perceived. Artemis and Eileithyia were considered beneficent daughters of Hera, the latter delivering new life within the oikos and the former as the younger sister and divine nurse who nourished the new life. A close and marked relationship between Hera -- as queen and mother of the gods who blesses households with children -- and these two goddesses as supporters of their mother would make a beneficial triad for expectant parents.

Apollon can also pulled into groupings with Artemis and Hera, and historically was in Thrake (likely in unity with the functions of his twin with whom he shares many characteristics and influences.) Such foci can be particularly good for giving offerings throughout the pregnancy for a healthy baby and easy delivery, and believe you me I was praying fervently to Artemis and Eileithyia during the birth of my daughter. Thanksgiving by parents can continue, though, not only for the successful longterm survival of children, in which context Apollon and Athena would also be honored, but also long after the birth of the children and even into successive generations even if only yearly on birthdays.

If you live in a very storm-prone area, you might consider establishing a shrine for Zeus, Hera Telkhinia and Apollon Telkinios as a safety measure for your oikos against the savaging winds and torrential rains; perhaps with Poseidon, too, if you are in a hurricane-prone area. These epithets of Apollon and Hera are particular to Rhodes, which is perhaps understandable, as islands tend to get the worst of violent weather, and are taken from the Telkines who were masters of weather and the seas. Of course, this not the only source for such associations for either of them as Apollon in the Iliad is addressed for bringing down the wall of the Hellenes by his winds with the rains of Zeus and the uprising waters of Poseidon. Likewise, Hera has very strong associations with the weather in her Orphic Hymn. Conversely, these four gods would be beneficial to worship together in places that tend to have drought, too.

Another pairing which individuals might find to be of some importance in their oikos is that of Hera and Aphrodite. In their worship, these two goddesses already share much in common in terms of titles and epithets. In fact, one epithet of Hera is "Aphrodite." Although Romans worshiped Venus, they seem to have given her little regard in terms of marital functions; rather, the worship was meant to offset interference of the goddess, which can ruin a happy marriage. This seems less the case with the relationship between Hera and Aphrodite -- although this is not to say that the domain of Aphrodite cannot occasionally be at odds with marital ideals. Instead, the primary motion of Aphrodite is geared towards marriage-as-a-goal, as we see in the Iliad when Zeus affectionately tells Aphrodite to concern herself more with making marriages than with involving herself in fighting in battles. Aphrodite as the receiver of new brides can also be seen in the myth of Kyrene in which the goddess prepares and welcomes Kyrene to her bridal bower. In fact, in terms of marriage, it seems that Aphrodite ought to be viewed as a more beneficial goddess, as the mother of harmony. It is, after all, by Aphrodite's girdle that Hera seduces her husband, and by her power that Hera and Zeus were wed and are reconciled to each other. Therefore, it can be very advantageous for an oikos to have a small shrine set up for Hera and Aphrodite as a pair, or as a triad with Zeus, in support of familial love and bonds, as well as a harmonious household.

Another possible pairing, one that was greatly appreciated in some parts of ancient Hellas, is that of Hera and her son Hephaistos. This may seem a bit strange to those who are familiar with the myth in which Hera was said to have thrown Hephaistos away as an infant, crippling him, for which Hephaistos later revenged himself on her. Yet a different myth attributes his crippling by being thrown to the earth after aiding his mother in escaping the chains that Zeus bound her in for her rebellion against his rule. These may of course be geographical variances, or could have been parallel myths existing side by side which would color the complexity of their relationship;

likely all children in some respect both resent and love their mothers at the same time. In Arkadia, according to Pausanias, Hephaistos was worshiped in his mother's temple at her side as "the war-like Zeus." It is apparent here that Hera's procreative relationship with Zeus is paralleled on a different level with the industriously creative relationship of Hera with her son. Hephaistos is creator extraordinaire, functioning on a different level than Zeus; Hephaistos primarily deals with the forms of things. Many of Hephaistos' constructs are things useful to war, such as armor and weaponry (Athena's armor, the bows of Apollon and Artemis). Hephaistos' industrial nature is very much tempered and influenced by Hera, more so than Zeus is influenced, even though she is his foremost advisor among the gods. Unlike with Zeus, with whom Hera shares rule and power, she has power directly over Hephaistos as his mother. For example, we find in the Iliad that Hephaistos turns the tides of war and oversets Xanthus, who was overwhelming the Hellenes by his floods, under the direction of his mother.

We see examples of the rule of the mother over her children again and again in myth. The son yields to and respects the will of his mother. In this context this pairing would probably be something that mothers appreciate for the smoothly operating oikos, while in the context of Hera's own cunning and industrious nature, her powerful pairing with Hephaistos could likely be very beneficial for business and other areas of work.

Regardless for what manner of shrine(s) you wish to establish in your household, those dedicated to Hera seem to have common themes. One may, or may not, have a statue as one's desires, finances or other capabilities allow. There are many lovely images of Hera available which can be framed as a central devotional image. One may also consider décor with peacock feathers or peacock imagery, as the peacock is her sacred animal (the many eyes of the peacock's feathers are those of Argos, the servant of Hera who Hermes slew). The peacock, incidentally, also draws her chariot through the heavens and

185

thus in both contexts it is perhaps one of the most common symbols associated with her. A bit less well-known is the crane, perhaps for its vigorous mating displays and habits. Another sacred animal that can be incorporated would be the cow, bull or ox, an image directly related to Hera herself as the great cow of the heavens and which would work really well in a joint shrine with several gods who have cattle sacred to them, such as Zeus, Poseidon, and Apollon. Other animals include the storm-bringing cuckoo, and lions, which are associated with both Zeus and Hera. Still other devotional items or representations include lotus flower imagery to represent Hera's lotus staff; apples to represent the Hesperides' apples that were gifted to Hera by Ge for her wedding; and the pomegranate, a sacred plant that she shares with Persephone.

Offerings of course can vary from person to person, but I prefer to give her sweet, light flower-scented incenses such as jasmine; even the Sri Lakshmi incense is quite pleasant. When giving her offerings together with Aphrodite, I will go to more heavy flower scents such as rose and gardenia, but veer away from very heavy scents such as musk or patchouli. Libations often consist of water sweetened with honey, or honeyed wine on special occasions. I try to encourage gifting Hera with sweet things, although not necessarily the decadent things I would give Aphrodite; it seems that Hera takes pleasure to the sweet little things. Among fresh flowers I have also found in personal experience that delicate flowers of classical bouquets are a favored offering.

In the end, how your shrine(s) develops and how frequently you give worship is up to you and how you wish to develop your relationship, and the relationship of your oikos, with Hera. I personally give her worship weekly at a minimum: on Thursdays with Zeus, and on Fridays with the other household goddesses. However, you may find your needs may require more frequent or less offerings and perhaps on different days of the week.

Regardless of how your worship continues from this point on, may Hera bestow her blessings upon you and your oikos, and may you find a greater relationship develop between yourself, your oikos, and our Queen.

A Song for the Gamelia
by Amanda Sioux Blake

Editor's Note: This poem was created as part of a Gamelia rite, which celebrates the marriage of Zeus and Hera.

Rich-haired Muses Nine, Dwellers on Helikon, I hail you.

I call you, Inspirers of arts and music, to attend to me,

And help me to tell the tale

Of the First Wedding,

The union of Mighty Zeus with Majestic Hera.

Lord Zeus, Ruler of Sky, I hail you.

Glorious King, august, mighty and invincible,

Thrower of lightning and causer of rain to fall,

Husband of queenly Hera, attend my song and hear my tale.

Queen Hera, Lady of Argos, I hail you.

Cow-eyed Goddess, always faithful,

Patroness of young brides and elder crones alike,

Wife of Lord Zeus, attend my song and hear my tale.

Years ago, before the present order had come to pass,

Young Zeus warred with his cruel father Kronos

And his Titan brothers.

Alongside the young Kretan God, his brothers by Kronos and Rhea,

Poseidon the Earth-Shaker, Haides the grim-faced God Below,

And their sisters, lovely fair-haired Demeter, gentle Hestia of the flames,

and the always Queenly Hera, fought against their severe father.

The war from which they emerged victorious lasted ten years.

Not so long in the lifespan of the Immortals,

But long enough

When spent hiding in dank, dark caves

And fighting fearsome battles with your own kin.

It was in this time of war and upheaval in the ranks of the Deathless Ones

That young Zeus Kourebates began to desire his sister Hera.

His sister was chaste and proper, earthy and beautiful like their sibling Demeter,

But not so wild and free. Queenly Hera, Co-Ruler of Sky, Patroness of Kings,

would not be easily taken.

Cow-eyed Hera was cordial to her brother, but wondered as to their future.

"Dearest brother Zeus," She said to him, "Your arm is strong, your visage handsome,

And your cause in this war just. But, virile as you are, you are easily ruled by your passion,

and I fear that passion may lead you astray."

"Ah," Replied Zeus "But my passion is my rudder. It is my passion

That led me to leave the safety of Krete; the nymphs there cared for me

And gave me all that I needed. But I knew the evils our father Kronos had wrought

And that my five siblings were stored up in his stomach, trapped and miserable, unable to fight for their freedom.

My passion to right this wrong led me back to Hellas.

My passion freed you and the others from captivity.

My passion enlisted the aid of Metis, Styx, and Mnemosyne, powerful Titanesses and valuable allies.

It is passion which has guided me to you, the green shore, where I will find welcome harbor and hospitably in your soft arms, as a sailor sore for the sight of land finds welcome in the bustling cities and green growing things of land. Let us lie together, and I will not forsake your bedside."

Lady Hera was not convinced by the Thunderer's honeyed words.

"Ah," the white-armed Goddess responded. "It is the way that your passion converted these Titanesses three to our cause that worries me! Your advances are not unwelcome, dear brother, but I must have assurances."

"What more can I say to convince you? What must I give you to assure you of my devotion? I shall give you rule of the heavens, and the fertility of earth you shall share with Demeter, if she does not object. I shall give you a crown of stars, and cities to rule as you see fit, and all Gods and Goddesses shall give honor to thy name."

Hera smiled coyly. "If you want me, you must marry me."

"Sister," Zeus replied, his brow knit in confusion, "What do you mean by this? There is no such word."

"It means," Hera told her brother. "That we will not simply lie together in the dark, and our pairing so be ended, nor be subject to the fickle flows of passion. Our bonding will be of stronger and more enduring stuff. You will swear, by your honor and by the River of Death, before all the Gods, to keep me and protect me. And I shall keep myself only for you, and not give myself to any other God. We will stand beside each other through good and bad, and one shall not desert the other. When the war is over and you have won, we shall live together as husband and wife. I will bare you children, and we will raise them together, not I alone as Demeter with her Kore. And this arrangement, this marriage, will not be limited to us. Others will follow our example, first Gods, and then mankind. Through marriage the world will be civilized, and the practice of it shall be my own special domain."

And so it was. Zeus swore it, to protect and stand beside her,

And Hera and Zeus lay together in love for the first time.

When the war of the Titans had ended and Kronos was cast into Tartaros,

All the Gods attended their golden wedding, and danced to the drums and feasted from the laden tables.

The beautiful bride and beaming bridegroom were a sight to behold,

No blemish in their Immortal faces, but only the shining glow

Of happiness at having found a mate that was truly their equal.

They say that their honeymoon lasted for three hundred years.

So the First Wedding occurred, and on this day of Gamelia,

We mortals of old celebrate the union of these two great Gods,

Our beloved King and Queen of Olympos

She and He Who Unite,

The Most Holy Ones,

Hera Zygia and Zeus Zygios.

HER PRIESTESS
by Kyria Skotas

Many of us spend our lives searching for connection, to the divine or to each other. We drive ourselves to the point of breaking, wishing for purpose and for direction. Often, we do not acknowledge it when it strikes.

These bonds are world changing. All shattering. They change who we are, if only a little, and they change how we interact with the world around us. They will always change the way we see the world, and our place within it.

I do not speak of bonds lightly, but in a deeper sense.

Bonds of soul and purpose. Bonds that transcend typical relationships, and petty rivalries.

It is in this way that becoming a priestess of the gods is often trivialized.

There are many roads that may lead a person to become dedicated to deity. Perhaps the individual wishes to serve the god alone, and spend his/her days away in prayer and offering, the soot and the stench of burnt wine clinging even as s/he purifies.

For others, it is a path of outer work that they seek, taking the words and the ways of their gods and sharing them with others. Speaking the names of their beloved to all who will listen. Doing good works in their name. Hosting rituals and rites for the communities around them.

Neither one is inclusive of all ways to serve the gods, and neither one is the whole of the truth. I dare say you could not have one path without some aspect of the other .... You could not dedicate yourself to public works in the name of your gods without first having some private practice of devotion through which you may understand them.

193

No matter the path and no matter the intention, there is an element of spirit bond that comes with being a priestess of a god.

My gods, the ones that I would call myself priestess to, are not gods that I have chosen. Which is not to say that choice is not an applicable facet, just that I did not. They have always been there, long before I knew precisely who they were or why I felt them. For whatever reason, in whatever way, I know that on some level somewhere within my chest, beneath my heart, wherein my soul sits between my ribs, there is an anchor, a tie that links me in a deeply profound way to my goddess.

And I know that even if I were to never again to speak her name, even if I were to never again pray or involve myself in ritual ... I know that she would still be there.

That is what I mean by the bonds that tie us to another: these deep-down heart- or soul-level bonds that have moved us inextricably within the purview of another being. This is what I feel with Hera. Somehow and in some way, I know that I am tied to her. In a way beyond words and for reasons millennia old and impossible to track by mortal eye alone.

But what does that mean in a practical aspect? What does it mean to be a priestess?

To be a priest of any god I think is to hold a level of devotion to them. No matter how it is that you express this truth or the level of dedication you are capable of offering. To be a priest of the gods is to hold them as a consistent truth within the soul and with a steady devotion.

I am frequently asked what it's like to be a priestess of Hera. And most of the time I just don't know what to say. It seems to me such a visceral and constant piece of who and what I am that I rarely think of it in terms separate from my own identity. It is a part of my life in a way that falls over all categories of my being. In belonging so completely with/to a deity, there is no part of our lives that is not affected by them. Our choices and our lives are still our own, but they are there with us in all aspects and we need only to look to find their mark upon our hearts. We need only to sit and let the world settle away, to see where they are and what their influence may be.

So when I say that my relationship with Hera is an inextricable piece of who I am, which I wholly believe to be the truth, that is not to say that I am not aware of the layers and the ways in which my life is changed or enhanced for my connection to her.

It is from this place of truth and solidity that I write of what it is to be her priestess.

Much of what it means to live with Hera is internal. A stillness, as with the sky before the thunder, as the sea's steady pull away from the shore before striking the earth. There is a quietness that I've grown accustomed to, so much so that I rarely notice it now. In that quiet is the buzzing of potential. In that quiet, still space, time drags on. I am often left in this stillness to consider my options, to reflect before choosing to speak. To step back from thoughtless reaction and to choose what will happen next. It is not the absence of emotion ... but the space where all emotion masses in the tangle and spin of a maelstrom. And in that center space it is easy to decide what next to do. To set aside the emotions that would consume control, or to choose to release them anyway.

This paints a very subdued picture of what it is to walk as Hera's priestess, all silk and veils and somber eyes. This is true, but beneath the surface, beneath the calm and beyond expectation, what I have most often been confronted with is not the need for quiet or for a delicate hand ... but the importance of action.

Every choice of word or silence is an action and worthy of every depth of consideration. To walk with Hera is to hold

195

the importance of every choice as though it were your last. Whether you fail in this, and whether you choose poorly or wise, it is in the action itself that the importance is placed. Silence itself can be powerful and righteous, but silence is not valuable if it is through the absence of action.

In these ways I'm most clearly conscious of the presence of Hera. Every time that I choose to act through fear, through pain or uncertainty, I know that I am standing in line with the path my goddess has set before me.

It is in the interest of action and effect that public work with Hera is most keenly displayed, though often still with the element of that silent stillness, that step aside and back from the constant chatter and torrential emotion that is the mortal world.

I knew before I ever had the chance to learn what it would mean, that I must walk the path of a public priestess for Hera. To be, for those who need it, that place of stillness that I have found with Hera. To bear for them the quiet space where action is revealed. To hold for them their secrets, their triumphs, and their pains. To stand as proof that action can be taken, even through pain and turmoil, and that glory is the result of those actions rightly upheld.

A CATHARTIC MOTHER'S DAY RITUAL
by Reverend Allyson Szabo

Background

In today's world, abuse is rampant. Mistreatment and outright neglect, painful punishments, and other nightmarish things happen to some as we grow up. When the world pauses to celebrate days like Mother's Day, those of us with abusive parents stop to ask ourselves, "What do we do?" For many, the answer is to ignore the holiday, or to lash out at others around us who may not be aware of our pain. This is counterproductive to a healthy spiritual life, though. Working through our feelings of abandonment, imperfection, guilt, and anger is very important, because it frees us to look at our bare souls. This ritual was created with the idea of releasing anger and hatred for your mother, allowing you to embrace motherhood in different and much more positive ways.

This is written up as a ritual for a single worshiper. Please feel free to adapt it for use with groups.

Set Up

Assemble all the items for the ritual: a bell or drum, wine, fresh water, a bowl for holding dirty water, a bowl for wine offerings, a branch, a candle or oil lamp, barley, a goblet, gifts for each of the Goddesses, and a small meal or feast (for after ritual). Have them ready, either on the altar or in the basket, as appropriate. The wine should be a bottle reserved just for that ritual. Any left over may be imbibed by the attendees, consider sharing with the Gods. Take time to bathe and completely cleanse the body and soul of any miasma.

Procession

Walk quietly, piously, into the ritual area. This marks the change from profane to sacred space. You may wish to ring a bell or beat a drum slowly to accompany the pace. Treat this as seriously as a procession with a hundred people!

Purification of the People

Just outside the sacred space, have a vessel of spring or sea water and a bowl waiting. You should wash your hands with the water, into the bowl (the water in the bowl is considered unclean, and so should not be touched). If more than one person is attending, the water is poured by the priestess, and the bowl is held by the priest. When by yourself, simply pausing to wash your hands in the bowl is fine, and the water should be disposed of away from your home or garden later.

Sanctification of Sacred Space

The remaining water in the vessel is used to sanctify the sacred space and the altar. Use a branch to scatter droplets of clean water around the entire area to be used during the ritual. As you walk, you can hum, sing, or recite a prayer. End the cleansing by sprinkling yourself, then take the offering basket up to the altar, and place it before or under it.

Ritual Lighting of Sacred Fire

The oil lamp/large candle is lit with a blessing to Hestia. This should be impromptu and not scripted. Other candles can be lit now, using a taper lit from the oil lamp.

Tossing of Barley

Scatter barley around the sacred space and altar, from a container of barley.

Preliminary Invocation

The priestess says:

You who are beyond death!

Goddesses of the Sacred Heights, the Earth around me, and the Great Below,

Hear me call!

Bless me with your presence,

Mothers of Gods,

for I wish to honor you.

Libations

Water and wine are mixed together in a wine glass or chalice. Pour the wine in first, filling the goblet half way, and then add the water. Then say:

Dear Hestia,

Receive this libation, and rejoice,

for your joy is mine this night.

Hestia, Goddess of the Hearth,

Guardian of the Home,

For you I pour out the first portion,

Accept and delight in my offerings.

For tender hearted Hecate,

Bright coiffed Lady of torches and light

Protector of childbirth and children,

Accept and delight in my offerings.

For Ox-Eyed Queen of Heaven,

Hera, thou Mother and wife,

Dark-eyed one, peacock-clad Goddess,

Accept and delight in my offerings.

Rhea, Mother of the Gods themselves,

Mysterious one, Great Mother,

Wise and wizened one,

Accept and delight in my offerings.

Celebration

On the altar, place a gift for each Goddess called, one at a time. Take a few moments to speak from the heart, saying what that Goddess means to you, and why. Explain to the Goddesses called that you are asking their aid in overcoming anger and negative emotions in regards to your own mother, and that your offerings are made with their help in mind. Enumerate your problems carefully, and bluntly. You may wish to have them written down, so that you can remember your issues. This can take as long or as short a time as you wish, but you should not be afraid to wallow just a little bit in your emotions. This is a good time to yell about your mother, and to allow the negative things to well up, and be cried out.

Last Libations

Once you are done, share some of the wine with the Goddesses, and then use the last part as a final libation to them. Say:

Receive these libations, and be kind,

for your joy is shared with me this night.

Hestia, Goddess of the Hearth,

Hecate, Mistress of Childbirth,

Hera, Queen of Heaven,

Rhea, Mother of the Gods,

For you I pour out the last portion,

In thanks for your help and your comfort.

Accept and delight in my offerings.

When you are done, quietly extinguish all candles and incense, if necessary. Clean up, and take any offerings outside, dispose of the dirty water, and generally tidy your altar space. Then, go have some food, with a small portion set aside for the Goddesses, in thanks.

BIBLIOGRAPHY:

Neokoroi – The Temple Keepers. Template for Noumenia Ritual.

Sannion's Sanctuary. Hellenic Polytheism.

Fairbanks, Arthur. A Handbook of Greek Religion.

Diasia/Chloaia. A ritual.

KATALLAGEIA
by Amanda Sioux Blake

Editor's Note: the Katallageia, celebrated in mid-November in the modern calendar, marks the reconciliation between Hera and her son, Hephaestus. The reasons for the latter's exile from Olympos vary in the surviving mythology. Celebrants are encouraged to delve deeply into the story, examining different versions, and considering what they can teach us about the Gods and about ourselves.

The altar is a coffee table, so it's long. It has one end set up for Hera, and one for Hephaistos. Hephaistos' image is covered with a cloth, as He has run away from Olympos and hidden Himself. Between Them is a khernips bowl, a small Libation bowl, a container of barley, some (unlit!) candles, and an empty plate for offerings. Don't light the candles until the part of the ritual when Hephaistos returns!

Behind these are set up a few small symbols of Dionysos, and a glass of wine, to symbolize His help in bringing Hephaistos back to Olympos. Don't make His image be the same size or scale as that of Hera or Hephaistos. It's important to thank Dionysos for His role, but He is not the focus of the festival.

After closing your eyes for a moment and centering yourself, step forward to the altar.

Barley Offering

"To the givers of life, Life." Sprinkle barley on the altar.

Cleansing

Place hands and face in water. Say: "With this holy water, I am cleansed. I enter the Presence of the Gods purified and free from pollution."

Pick up khernips bowl. Walk around the altar or circle, and while sprinkling water onto the ground say: "You are pure! You are pure! With this holy water, this is now sacred ground. You are pure! You are pure!"

Walk around the circle one more time, and have the worshippers wash their hands and face in the water while you hold the bowl. As they are doing so, say: "With this holy water, you are cleansed." Do this with each one, then replace the bowl at its previous spot on the altar.

Prayer to Hera

(From Orphic Hymn 16: To Hera)

Stand before the altar, palms raised to the sky. Say: "O royal Hera, of majestic mien, aerial-formed, divine, Zeus' blessed queen, throned in the bosom of cerulean air, the race of mortals is thy constant care. The cooling gales thy power alone inspires, which nourish life, which every life desires.

"Mother of showers and winds, from thee alone, producing all things, mortal life is known: all natures share thy temperament divine, and universal sway alone is thine, with sounding blasts of wind, the swelling sea and rolling rivers roar when shook by thee.

"Come, blessed Goddess, famed almighty queen, with aspect kind, rejoicing and serene."

204

Plea to Dionysos

"O freedom-loving Dionysos, help us now! Hephaistos in His anger has trapped Queen Hera in a throne of steel, and fled from Olympos' snowy peaks. With Him go His gifts to mankind. Bright fire to warm us and cook our food, technology to make our lives easier, and even pretty jewelry and adornments, pleasant to the eye. None can exist without the Smith. Though many people take Him for granted today, or ignore His existence completely, our world cannot exist without Him!

"Proud Dionysos, go to the Wounded Worker, ply Him with Your sweet wine until His heart becomes peaceful once more, and bring Hephaistos back to Olympos where he so rightly belongs!"

Revealing of Hephaistos

Remove the cloth covering the image of Hephaistos. Joyously shout: "Hephaistos has returned! Light appears unto the world again! Fire will burn and machines will run! Praise be to the Mighty Smith, creator of many wonders for mankind!"

Light the Candles and Incense

(From Orphic Hymn 66: To Hephaestus)

"Strong, mighty Hephaistos, bearing splendid light, unwearied fire, with flaming torrents bright: strong-handed, deathless, and of art divine, pure element, a portion of the world is thine: all-taming artist, all-diffusive power, tis thine, supreme, all substance to devour: aither, sun, moon, and stars, light pure and clear, for these thy lucid parts [of fire] to men appear.

"To thee all dwellings, cities, tribes belong, diffused through mortal bodies, rich and strong. Hear, blessed power, to holy rites incline, and all propitious on the incense shine: suppress the rage of fire's unwearied frame, and still preserve our nature's vital flame."

Thanksgiving and Offerings

In a loud voice, proclaim: "We offer our thanks also to the Ivy-Twined One, Bright Semele's child, Dionysos the Two-Horned, He of Two Mothers. Thanks be to Zeus's mighty son, for His sweet wine has calmed the fiery temper and softened the metal heart. Let it be known through out the lands, that this time, it was drunkenness that saved the world!"

Offer the fish to Hephaistos, the pomegranate to Hera, and the wine to Dionysos.

Cut a fat, juicy looking piece of fish and put it on the plate on the altar. Say: "Famed Hephaistos, the Sooty God, who creates beauty from ugliness, we offer You this baked fish, in remembrance of Your childhood among the waves, of Thetys and Doris, those sea-Goddesses who bought You up. May our offerings please You."

Place slices of the pomegranates onto the plate. To avoid mess, cut the pieces out beforehand. Say: "Glorious Hera, Queen of Heaven, arrayed in peacock feathers, we offer You Your sacred pomegranates, the fruit of marriage, in honor that You are Zygia, the Uniter, who makes one being from two, and strengthens the bonds of family. May our offerings please You."

Pour some of wine into libation bowl. Say: "O Dionysos of the wine-casks, we will share with You this glass of wine, light and sweet, to remind ourselves that life cannot be all business; we must enjoy all the Gods give to us. We must stop to smell the roses. Let us remember, also, that life is too short for grudges, for hatred or revenge, for all too soon we who take our journey Underground."

Turn back to the altar. Say: "And now, we the celebrants, the worshipers, will take our portion of this sacred meal. Lady Hera, Hard-working Hephaistos, and Laughing Dionysos, we humbly invite You to dine with us tonight. May You hear our prayers, and be kind towards us. In community we begin. In community we end. Khairete."

Worshipers partake of the fish and pomegranates and wine. Now feast! Be merry, and be kind to each other.

BY HER GRACE

by Jolene Dawe

I got married before I was ready to. I hesitate to say "before I should have," because in the end it's worked out very well. I joke a bit that it was more of an elopement than anything. "Hey, what do you say we get married?" "Sure!" and then it was poof, I was wed. I didn't talk to my family about it until after, I didn't talk to many of my friends about it until after.

Perhaps I should mention here that my marriage vows were given to my God, not to a mortal spouse, and so for some of my family as well as for some people in general, my marriage doesn't count as a marriage, per se. For me, in the beginning, it both did and it didn't ... and this is what set me up for the heartache that was to follow. (I'll point out too that, while the marriage vows were a bit ... sudden, I already had years of devotion to this God as a foundation to build upon.)

I grew up in a "broken" home. My father was an alcoholic (and not a happy drunk, mind you), my mother coped the best she could, and I had a major hand in raising my younger brother. If you've grown up in a house with substance abuse, I don't have to explain the lovely baggage it can give you, and if you haven't, I don't know that I have the words to make you understand. I saw my father treating my mother horribly, and my mother staying around to take it. I did not grow up with a healthy opinion of marriage. I didn't really grow up wanting to get married, although I thought eventually I would. The upside to this sort of upbringing is that I came out of it with a rather strong opinion about family. Family is what you create, family is not defined solely by blood. I have people in my family who are connected through blood ties first, but there are people with shared genetics that I do not count as family, and the majority of my family is not connected through blood -- a large part of my family isn't human at all.

This is the baggage I was already trying to sort through and get rid of before I got married. I was working on being able to see the panic attacks before they started. I was working on being able to be in crowds without completely shutting down. I was making an effort to keep apathy at bay. I was pushing my awareness to new heights with a yoga practice. The foundation was there.

By the time I gave my God my "I do" I was expecting something to change between us, though honestly I had no idea what that thing would be. I didn't think I was suddenly this grand, important person, and I really had no desire to be. I wanted (and want) to live my life quietly. I wanted to study and spend time with my Gods and write and do small things. I felt a crushing guilt that I didn't want to achieve more, but wanting to want to do something is ultimately useless as far as motivation goes. After getting married, I wanted ... something. And because that nameless something didn't manifest, things went south, pretty fast. If my marriage had been a marriage with a mortal spouse, my treatment of them would have danced pretty close to verbal abuse. I accused my Husband of setting up an elaborate joke, to which I was the punchline, because clearly that's all I could be good for. I tried very hard to get Him to see His folly in not striking me dead. I broke shrines. I called Him names. I deserved nothing but contempt, nothing but disdain, or at the very least neglect. When I woke up every morning, aware of my Gods in my life, I was not grateful. I was repelled and disgusted -- not with Them, but in Their allowing me to be aware of Them, and the holder of my marriage vows bore the brunt of this. It was ugly, it was bad, it was absolutely wretched -- and I'm not sure I would have been able to purge myself of the baggage I carried quite as effectively any other way.

But then what? So I could point to these pieces of myself and see where they'd come from, and why. So I could distance myself compassionately from my emotions and not be a slave to them. So I could say with a straight face and with utter seriousness that I was married, despite my lack of a mortal husband. What do I do with these things, and how could I begin to take myself seriously as a wife? What did being a wife even mean for someone like me? In those first few steps of crawling back to being "good," I have to admit I contemplated: did I even want this? Would it be better to go back to not calling this a marriage? Did that term matter, really?

I am a big supporter of Words Meaning Things, and 'wife' meant something more than simply 'devoted-to', to me. It meant building a life with. It meant taking in this God to be the center of my life, it meant agreeing that my Divine Family was also as much my immediate family as it could become. Knowing this, I still had a very hard time taking myself seriously as a wife. I felt, continually, as though I was a little girl playing house. Except, I wasn't. I was an adult, with more life experience behind me even in my early twenties that some people had until much later. I'd already raised a child, and I was helping to raise another. I started working and supporting a household financially while still in high school. I looked younger than I was, and often people dismissed me as being a child, because they couldn't see these experiences I'd already had. It was easy to not take myself seriously, but I needed to move beyond that.

It wasn't anything I meant to do. I reached a place where it was time to start shoring up the foundation again, this time with things that would serve me well, for the rest of my life. I prayed. I meditated. I reached, and I reached, and I held myself open .. and I found myself drawn to first Aphrodite and then Hera.

It shouldn't have been too surprising. When I'd given my Husband my vows, I also gave them to Zeus and Hera. "Here. These are the things I promise. See them, witness them, hold them, help me to uphold them." It made sense in my polytheistic mind both because They are my Husband's Family and because of Their place, traditionally, within the Hellenic pantheon. Still, as I found myself thinking more and more

210

about Hera, I was surprised. And, I'm ashamed to say, a bit reluctant. My knowledge of Hera extended only as far as the caricature of Her that comes through: a jealous, insecure wife whose husband runs around on her; a powerless woman who must console herself with whatever petty revenge she can muster. Later, I would learn how this image of Hera does not mesh with the evidence we have of Her cults. Later, I would come to know how nuanced and complex Her worship was and how generous She is.

At Her direction, I looked into places I otherwise might not have. My marriage wasn't typical; why would I look into common areas of hardship that typical newlyweds faced? Except, when I did, I found things that could help me. No, it may not fit exactly, but there were tools to be had, experiences to learn from. I wasn't the first woman to have had an already established friendship that became a marriage a bit unexpectedly, and with mortals this could create problems. Established roles were shaken up. Expectations that weren't fully named were left partially fulfilled, or unfulfilled, and disappointment or confusion or poor communication resulted. These things so easily poison into resentment. Resentment left to fester can be such a horrible, damaging thing. If this could happen with mortals, why couldn't it happen in my case? I'm mortal, after all, with a mortal's shortsightedness and impatience.

A religious marriage, as opposed to a purely secular one, is still a contract of sorts. I jumped into mine without ironing out details, and maybe I couldn't have ironed out the details beforehand, but I didn't even have any idea what the details were there. That there could be details. That there would be details. It certainly wasn't fair for me to become upset when things didn't change as I expected them to. (I wanted some Great Work to be announced for me, even though I also wanted to do small things and not Big Things, and when that wound up being "Keep doing as you are," ... well. It was bad. I was bad.)

211

So, I looked at other marriages, mortal and otherwise. I looked at my own marriage. I looked at marriages throughout history, in different cultures and time periods. I looked back at my own marriage. I looked at marriages within mythology. I looked at marriages between religious people and I looked at secular marriages. I looked at open marriages and poly marriages and monogamous marriages. I looked at all the different ways you could be married. I looked at Zeus and Hera, and Their complicated partnership. I looked at it with an eye toward the literal, and an eye toward the metaphoric. And I realized, finally, finally, that my marriage would be what I helped make it be. That it was between my Husband and I, what would work, what wouldn't work, what we called it. It was absolutely imperative that I take myself seriously, because it was my responsibility to do so, and I had no business giving anyone else the power to take this role from me.

It sounds, written up, like such a small thing. The words can't do it justice. Hera graced my life with Her presence, and because of Her generosity, my marriage was able to mend. I was able to mend. I leapt into this marriage likely before I was ready, but I can't see how I ever could have been ready without having gone through this. It is because of Hera that I can say "wife" and mean it. It is because of Hera that I have confidence in what I know of myself, of what I know of my Husband. It is through Her influence that I was able to bring back into my awareness the sacredness of this life, that I was able to weave together the mundane and the sacred in such a way that my relationship now flourishes. With Her guidance, I was able to gain a greater sense of openness with my Husband. With Her blessing, I was given a deeper understanding of the mystery of marriage, and able to make this the center of my life. Words can never convey the depth of my gratitude.

This is very uncomfortable to share, but I'm sharing it because I think it's important. Who I gave my vows to doesn't matter here so much as the fact that I gave them, and when the marriage suffered, it was Hera who helped me find my footing and guided me to a healthy place upon which to build. I believe it's of the utmost importance that one goes into a marriage mindfully, with the intent that the marriage be defined by those in the marriage, and by no one else. And, I believe that when there is doubt, when there is confusion or misunderstanding, it is important to turn to our Gods for aid. And, I believe that when we are blessed by Their aid, we must sing Their praise and share our stories. So, this is me, doing that.

Hail Hera

Glorious Goddess

Shine Your blessings down upon the brides

Upon the grooms

A marriage, a decision, every day

To be yoked together

To live together, to grow together

You have granted me the ability to make that decision

Every day, again and again.

My soul cries out in joy, at this gift You have given me

To love, to live, to continually give of myself

These things I can do because of Your grace upon me

Hera, for this You have my undying gratitude

For this, I will always offer You praise

Goddess, keep my vows close to You and help me to remember

Hail, Hera

APPENDIX A: ANCIENT HYMNS

Homeric Hymn XII (To Hera)

I sing of golden-throned Hera whom Rhea bare. Queen of the immortals is she, surpassing all in beauty: she is the sister and the wife of loud-thundering Zeus, —the glorious one whom all the blessed throughout high Olympus reverence and honor even as Zeus who delights in thunder.

(The Homeric Hymns and Homerica with an English Translation by Hugh G. Evelyn-White. Cambridge, MA., Harvard University Press; London, William Heinemann Ltd. 1914.)

Orphic Hymn XV (To Juno)

The Fumigation from Aromatics.

O Royal Juno [Hera] of majestic mien, aerial-form'd, divine, Jove's [Zeus'] blessed queen,

Thron'd in the bosom of cærulean air, the race of mortals is thy constant care.

The cooling gales thy pow'r alone inspires, which nourish life, which ev'ry life desires.

Mother of clouds and winds, from thee alone producing all things, mortal life is known:

All natures share thy temp'rament divine, and universal sway alone is thine.

With founding blasts of wind, the swelling sea and rolling rivers roar, when shook by thee.

Come, blessed Goddess, fam'd almighty queen, with aspect kind, rejoicing and serene.

(The Hymns of Orpheus. Translated by Thomas Taylor (1792). University of Pennsylvania Press, 1999.)

16. To Hera

Incense: Aromatic Herbs

You are ensconced in darksome hollows, and airy is your form, O Hera,

Queen of all and blessed consort of Zeus.

You send soft breezes to mortals such as nourish the soul,

And, O mother of rains, you nurture the winds and give birth to all.

Without you there is neither life nor growth;

And, mixed as you are in the air we venerate, you partake of all,

And of all you are queen and mistress.

You toss and turn with the rushing wind.

May you, O blessed goddess and many-named queen of all,

Come with kindness and joy on your lovely face.

(*The Orphic Hymns*. Translated by Apostolos N. Athanassakis. Johns Hopkins University Press, 2013.)

APPENDIX B: RECOMMENDED READING

Cratylus, in *Plato in Twelve Volumes*, Vol. 12 translated by Harold N. Fowler. Cambridge, MA, Harvard University Press; London, William Heinemann Ltd., 1921.

The Cult of Divine Birth in Ancient Greece, by Marguerite Rigoglioso. Palgrave MacMillan, 2011.

d'Aulaire's *Book of Greek Mythology*, by Edgar and Ingri Parin d'Aulaire. Random House Children's Books, 1992.

Description of Greece, by Pausanias. English Translation by W.H.S. Jones, Litt.D., and H.A. Ormerod, M.A., in 4 Volumes. Cambridge, MA, Harvard University Press; London, William Heinemann Ltd., 1918.

Earth's Daughters: Stories of Women in Classical Mythology, by Betty Bonham Lies. Fulcrum Publishing, 1999.

The Glory of Hera: Greek Mythology and the Greek Family, by Phillip Elliott Slater. Princeton University Press, 1992.

The Goddess: Mythological Images of the Feminine, by Christine Downing. iUniverse, 2007.

Goddesses, Wives, Whores, and Slaves: Women in Classical Antiquity, by Sarah B Pomeroy. Knopf Doubleday, 1992.

Hera: The Goddess and Her Glory, by George O'Conner. First Second, 2011.

The Homeric Hymns and Homerica with an English Translation, by Hugh G. Evelyn-White. Cambridge, MA., Harvard University Press; London, William Heinemann Ltd. 1914.

The Hymns of Orpheus, translated by Thomas Taylor (1792). University of Pennsylvania Press, 1999.

The Library of Apollodorus, with an English Translation by Sir James George Frazer, F.B.A., F.R.S. in 2 Volumes. Cambridge, MA, Harvard University Press; London, William Heinemann Ltd. 1921.

Lost Goddesses of Early Greece: A Collection of Pre-Hellenic Myths, by Charlene Spretnak. Beacon, 1992.

The Myth of the Goddess: Evolution of an Image, by Anne Baring and Jules Cashford. Penguin Group, 1993.

The Orphic Hymns, translated by Apostolos N. Athanassakis. Johns Hopkins University Press, 2013.

Treasury of Greek Mythology: Classic Stories of Gods, Goddesses, Heroes and Monsters, by Donna Jo Napoli and Christina Balit. National Geographic Society, 2011.

Virgin Mother Crone: Myths and Mysteries of the Triple Goddess, by Donna Wilshire. Inner Traditions, 1993.

We Goddesses: Athena, Aphrodite, Hera, by Doris Orgel and Marilee Heyer. DK Publishing, 1999.

Zeus: Lord of the Sky by Doris Gates and Robert Handville. Penguin Group, 1982.

APPENDIX C: OUR CONTRIBUTORS

Jonathon Agathokles began his journey into Hellenismos during the late spring of 2009 after finding out about it's existence via wikipedia. This followed several years of disappointment and spiritually unsatisfying dabbling with eclectic neopaganism, and even more years of fascination with ancient mythologies and religions, especially the Hellenic and Roman religions. Because of these past experiences Jonathan leans very much towards the reconstructionist side of the religious spectrum. Jonathan also started blogging about the religion and his experiences in it on the blog A Young Flemish Hellenist, and enjoys learning more about ancient Hellenic religion, mythology, culture, customs, etc. He is also learning the ancient Hellenic language.

Christa A. Bergerson has adored and worshipped the Roman-Greco-Egyptian Gods since she was a wee, precocious tot. She is an occultist, an environmentalist, and a spiritualist, in no particular order. Her intuited poetry has appeared in *Waters of Life: A Devotional Anthology for Isis and Serapis*, *Bearing Torches: A Devotional Anthology for Hekate*, *Lady Churchill's Rosebud Wristlet*, *Abyss & Apex Magazine of Speculative Fiction*, *The Beltane Papers*, and *Illumen*, among several other publications. Feel free to contact her at carmentaeternus@comcast.net for astral and/or sublunary communication.

Frances Billinghurst is an initiated witch and High Priestess of an active coven based in Adelaide, South Australia. Her interest in the occult and all things magical, as well as folklore and mythology, spans some 20+ years. A prolific writer, her articles have appeared in an increasing number of publications worldwide including *Llewellyn's Witch's Calendar*, *Unto Herself: A Devotional Anthology to Independent Goddesses*, *Witchy Magic and The Faeries Queens*. Her own book, *Dancing the Sacred Wheel: A Journey through the Southern Sabbats*, was published in 2012, with limited copies available from the author. For further information, write to PO Box 2451, Salisbury Downs SA 5108, Australia or visit the Temple of the Dark Moon's web site templedarkmoon.com.

Amanda Sioux Blake is the keeper of the Temple of Athena the Savior, Alexandrian Tradition, and the author of *Ink In My Veins: A Collection of Contemporary Pagan Poetry and Songs of Praise: Hymns to the Gods of Greece*. She is currently working on the forthcoming *Journey to Olympos: A Modern Spiritual Odyssey*.

A self-labeled history geek, she has taught classes on Greek Mythology and has written the coursework for "Olympos in Egypt", an introduction to the unique hybrid culture and spiritually that grew up in Alexandria, Egypt in the Hellenistic Age. If you are interested, email her at starsong_dragon@yahoo.com. She also runs an online T-shirt store specializing in Greek and Egyptian designs, as well as general Pagan and fantasy, which can be found here http://www.cafepress.com/other_world.

Chelsea Luellon Bolton has a BA and a MA in Religious Studies from the University of South Florida (2009). She has been dedicated to the Ancient Egyptian Goddess Aset for a decade. She is currently translating ancient hymns for hymnal books for Aset and Sekhmet. She is also working on a devotional book and an oracle book for Aset. She has been previously published in some anthologies from Bibliotheca Alexandrina. She can be found at her blog http://fiercelybrightone.wordpress.com/

Diane "Emerald" Bronowicz is a Hellenic-focused Neo-Pagan from Pittsburgh, PA. She belongs to a traditional Wiccan coven and to Sassafras Grove, her local congregation of Ár nDraíocht Féin: A Druid Fellowship (ADF). ADF is an international, Neo-Pagan church whose practice is rooted in the history and mythology of the cultures across the Indo-European spectrum, and Emerald currently serves as its Bard Laureate. She has also served as the Chief and Secretary of ADF's Hellenic Kin (Oi

Asproi Koukouvayies: The White Owls Kin) and as Chief of ADF's Bardic Guild. She wrote this invocation to Hera for her wedding ceremony which was held in June 2012.

Rebecca Buchanan is the editor-in-chief of Bibliotheca Alexandrina and the editor of *Eternal Haunted Summer*, a Pagan literary ezine. Her works have appeared in *Bards and Sages Quarterly, Cliterature, Datura, Hex Magazine, Linguistic Erosion, Luna Station Quarterly, Mandragora*, and other venues.

Edward P. Butler received his Ph.D. from the New School for Social Research for his dissertation "The Metaphysics of Polytheism in Proclus". More information about his work can be found at henadology.wordpress.com/.

Hester Butler-Ehle (Hearthstone) is a pagan, heathen, polytheist and free-form druid who has honored the Greek gods for well over a decade.

Jolene Dawe is a polytheist devoted to Poseidon and Odin. She is the author of *Treasures from the Deep*, a collection of Poseidon's myths retold, and *The Fairy Queen of Spencer's Butte and Other Tales*. She lives in the Pacific Northwest with her partner, a small horde of cats, one small dog, and three spunky spinning wheels. You can find her online at
http://thesaturatedpage.wordpress.com/ and
http://naiadis.wordpress.com/

Katherine Meyers Dickens opted not to provide a biography.

Aldrin Fauni-Tanos identifies as a Hellenistic Pagan, although he does not think twice to participate in the rites of other traditions whenever he can. Of all the Gods on Olympos, he holds Hermes, Dionysos, Apollon, Ares, Athene, and Hera closest to his heart. He loves languages, ancient history, and dancing. He also blogs at www.undertwotrees.wordpress.com and is an associate editor at www.dialectsarchive.com.

Jason Ross Inczauskis completed his Masters degree in Plant Biology, and is residing close to Chicago, Illinois. He currently lives in a small apartment with his love, Tabitha, and more books and dolls than you can shake a stick at. He has worshipped Athena since the year 2000, and gradually came to worship the other Hellenic deities as well, officially converting to Hellenismos in 2010. When asked about his spiritual path, he may refer to himself as a Hellene, a Hellenic, or Greek Pre-Orthodox, depending on who's asking and his mood at the time, though he always follows it with the caveat: 'but not a very good one'. He is the editor for *Shield of Wisdom: A Devotional Anthology in Honor of Athena*. His devotional writing has also appeared in *He Epistole* and *Eternal Haunted Summer*, as well as several books, including *From Cave to Sky: A Devotional Anthology in Honor of Zeus*, *Guardian of the Road: A Devotional Anthology in Honor of Hermes*, *Harnessing Fire: A Devotional Anthology in Honor of Hephaestus*, *Out of Arcadia: A Devotional Anthology in Honor of Pan*, *Unto Herself: A Devotional Anthology for Independent Goddesses*, *The Scribing Ibis: An Anthology of Pagan Fiction in Honor of Thoth*, and *The Shining Cities: An Anthology of Pagan Science Fiction*.

Raven Kaldera has opted not to provide a biography.

Robert F. Koenig has a degree in Popular Culture, and through many ongoing studies of different religions, completed a degree in Mystical Christianity through the Universal Life Church. He has also studied Mary Magdalene with Esoteric Mystery School. As a husband and father he also contributes to many volunteer groups in his Long Island community. He enjoys the Hellenic Gods and Goddesses and seeks to bring the Divine Feminine on the same par with the Divine Masculine. As a singer-songwriter, Bob has many musical releases from pop to country.

Heather Kohser experiences the Divine by hand-feeding chickadees, talking with plant devas, shamanic journeys, ecstatic dancing, flirting with owls, adventuring with her dogs, communing with fossils, and many other pleasures that cultivate whimsy. Pediatric Nurse by night and eclectic pagan Reiki Practitioner by day, Heather fits in some writing amidst her many other joys in life. Her articles on Goddess thealogy and channeling feminist heroines have been published in *Goddess Magazine* and *Unto Herself: A Devotional Anthology for Independent Goddesses*, as well as the forth-coming anthology, *Shield of Wisdom*. She lives on an island in Lake Champlain with her beloved wife and their five fur-babies. To read more about her magical world check out her blog http://ofeskiesandalchemy.blogspot.com/

Galina Krasskova is a Heathen priest and Northern Tradition shaman who is currently pursuing a PhD in classics. She is the author of over a dozen books and may be found lurking and causing trouble at http://krasskova.weebly.com.

Jennifer Lawrence likes doing things the hard way, which explains most of how her life has turned out. She has earned a B.A. in English (concentration in Literature, specialization in Medieval Lit) and a B.S. in Criminal Justice. Her interests include history, gardening, herbalism, mythology and fairy tales, hiking, camping, and the martial arts. A multi-trad pagan, she has followed the gods of Greece, Ireland, and the Northlands for decades now; aside from membership with Ár nDraíocht Féin, she is also the steward for the state of Illinois for The Troth, Treasurer for Hellenion, and a member of Ord Brigideach. She lives with five cats, an overgrown garden full of nature spirits, and a houseful of gargoyles somewhere outside of Chicago.

Gerri Leen lives in Northern Virginia and originally hails from Seattle. She has a collection of short stories, Life Without Crows, out from Hadley Rille Books, and over fifty stories and poems published in such places as: *She Nailed a Stake Through His Head*, *Sword and Sorceress XXIII*, *Dia de los Muertos*, *Return to Luna*, *Sniplits*, *Triangulation: Dark Glass*, *Sails & Sorcery*, and *Paper Crow*. She also is editing an anthology of speculative fiction and poetry from Hadley Rille Books that will benefit homeless animals. Visit gerrileen.com to see what else she's been up to.

P. Sufenas Virius Lupus is a metagender person, and one of the founding members of the Ekklesía Antínoou –- a queer, Graeco-Roman-Egyptian syncretist reconstructionist polytheist group dedicated to Antinous, the deified lover of the Roman Emperor Hadrian, and related deities and divine figures –- as well as a contributing member of Neos Alexandria and a practicing Celtic Reconstructionist pagan in the traditions of gentlidecht and filidecht, as well as Romano-British, Welsh, and Gaulish deity devotions. Lupus is also dedicated to several land spirits around the area of North Puget Sound and its islands. Lupus' work (poetry, fiction, and essays) has appeared in a number of Bibliotheca Alexandrina devotional volumes, as well as Ruby Sara's anthologies *Datura* (2010) and *Mandragora* (2012), Inanna Gabriel and C. Bryan Brown's *Etched Offerings* (2011), Lee Harrington's *Spirit of Desire: Personal Explorations of Sacred Kink* (2010), and Galina Krasskova's *When the Lion Roars* (2011). Lupus has also written several full-length books, including *The Phillupic Hymns* (2008), *The Syncretisms of Antinous* (2010), *Devotio Antinoo: The Doctor's Notes, Volume One* (2011), *All-Soul, All-Body, All-Love, All-Power: A TransMythology* (2012), *A Garland for Polydeukion* (2012), and *A Serpent Path Primer* (2012), with more on the way.

Lykeia is a multimedia artist, and is particularly devoted to Apollon.

Jessica Orlando opted not to provide a biography.

Brenda Kyria Skotas is a High Priestess of the Bloodroot Honey Priestess Tribe, a Pan-Dianic tradition in the SF Bay Area. A dedicated priestess of Hera, she prides herself on holding safe space for others to heal and find their own strength as sovereign women. In practice, she is an animist and Hellenic polytheist with a reverent respect for those who have gone before. A practical and fearless witch, Brenda has created her own path from the remnants of personal experience, failure, a love for fairy tale trickery and the use of her own hands. Fiber arts, cordials, and scavenged tools are an oft seen part of what takes place before her hearth. You can find more of her writing on her blog, smokefromthetemple.wordpress.com.

Melia Suez is an eclectic Hellenic polytheist who lives high up in the Rocky Mtns with her son and husband. She was the editor for *From Cave To Sky: A Devotional Anthology in Honor of Zeus*. Her writings are a tribute not only to the chosen subject but also to Hermes.

Rev. Allyson Szabo is an interfaith minister, priestess, and author. Her book *Longing For Wisdom: The Message of the Maxims* came out in 2006 and was published by *Bibliotheca Alexandrina*. Several of her works have appeared in the BA anthologies. She writes for her blog, The Temple of Joy (ambertemple.blogspot.com/) and can be found on FaceBook and G+.

Suzanne Thackston is a Hellenic polytheist, a Demetrian priestess, a former homeschooling mom of now-grown sons, a tender of old horses, a devoted but inept gardener, a reader, a seeker, a dreamer and an endlessly curious student of the world, the universe and everything.

Alexis Solvey Viorsdottir has opted not to provide a biography.

Jack Wren is not a Hellenist, but believes that Hera deserves more attention than she gets in the modern world. He blogs at jackadreams.info.

About Bibliotheca Alexandrina

Ptolemy Soter, the first Makedonian ruler of Egypt, established the library at Alexandria to collect all of the world's learning in a single place. His scholars compiled definitive editions of the Classics, translated important foreign texts into Greek, and made monumental strides in science, mathematics, philosophy and literature. By some accounts over a million scrolls were housed in the famed library, and though it has long since perished due to the ravages of war, fire, and human ignorance, the image of this great institution has remained as a powerful inspiration down through the centuries.

To help promote the revival of traditional polytheistic religions we have launched a series of books dedicated to the ancient gods of Greece and Egypt. The library is a collaborative effort drawing on the combined resources of the different elements within the modern Hellenic and Kemetic communities, in the hope that we can come together to praise our gods and share our diverse understandings, experiences and approaches to the divine.

A list of our current and forthcoming titles can be found on the following page. For more information on the Bibliotheca, our submission requirements for upcoming devotionals, or to learn about our organization, please visit us at neosalexandria.org.

Sincerely,

The Editorial Board of the Library of Neos Alexandria

BIBLIOTHECA ALEXANDRINA

CURRENT TITLES

Written in Wine:

> *A Devotional Anthology for Dionysos*

Dancing God:

> *Poetry of Myths and Magicks*

Goat Foot God

Longing for Wisdom:

> *The Message of the Maxims*

The Phillupic Hymns

Unbound:

> *A Devotional Anthology for Artemis*

Waters of Life:

> *A Devotional Anthology for Isis and Serapis*

Bearing Torches:

> *A Devotional Anthology for Hekate*

Queen of the Great Below:

> *An Anthology in Honor of Ereshkigal*

From Cave to Sky:

> *A Devotional Anthology in Honor of Zeus*

Out of Arcadia:

> *A Devotional Anthology for Pan*

Anointed:

A Devotional Anthology for the Deities of the Near and Middle East

The Scribing Ibis:

An Anthology of Pagan Fiction in Honor of Thoth

Queen of the Sacred Way:

A Devotional Anthology in Honor of Persephone

Unto Herself:

A Devotional Anthology for Independent Goddesses

The Shining Cities:

An Anthology of Pagan Science Fiction

Guardian of the Road:

A Devotional Anthology in Honor of Hermes

Harnessing Fire:

A Devotional Anthology in Honor of Hephaestus

Beyond the Pillars:

An Anthology of Pagan Fantasy

FORTHCOMING TITLES

A Mantle of Stars:
>*A Devotional Anthology in Honor of the Queen of Heaven*

Crossing the River:
>*An Anthology in Honor of Sacred Journeys*

Potnia:
>*An Anthology in Honor of Demeter*

Shield of Wisdom:
>*A Devotional Anthology in Honor of Athena*

Megaloi Theoi:
>*A Devotional Anthology for the Diskouroi*
>*and Their Families*

Sirius Rising:
>*A Devotional Anthology for Cynocephalic Deities*

Made in the USA
Middletown, DE
22 May 2015